At Sylvan, we believe that developing a strong vocabulary is among life's most important skills, and we're glad you've chosen our resources to help your child build this crucial knowledge. An effective vocabulary is a toolkit that readies your child for school and beyond.

At Sylvan, vocabulary instruction uses a step-by-step process with research-based and thought-provoking lessons. With success, students become more confident. With increasing confidence, students build even more success. That's why our Sylvan workbooks aren't like the others; we're laying out the roadmap for learning.

Included with your purchase is a coupon for a discount on our in-center service. As your child continues his academic journey, your local Sylvan Learning Center can partner with your family to ensure that your child remains a confident, successful, and independent learner.

The Sylvan Team

Sylvan Learning Center.
Unleash your child's potential here.

No matter how big or small the academic challenge, every child has the ability to learn. But sometimes children need help making it happen. Sylvan believes every child has the potential to do great things. And, we know better than anyone else how to tap into that academic potential so that a child's future really is full of possibilities. Sylvan Learning Center is the place where your child can build and master the learning skills needed to succeed and unlock the potential you know is there.

The proven, personalized approach of our in-center programs deliver unparalleled results that other supplemental education services simply can't match. Your child's achievements will be seen not only in test scores and report cards but outside the classroom as well. And when he starts achieving his full potential, everyone will know it. You will see a new level of confidence come through in everything he does and every interaction he has.

How can Sylvan's personalized in-center approach help your child unleash his potential?

• Starting with our exclusive Sylvan Skills Assessment®, we pinpoint your child's exact academic needs.

• Then we develop a customized learning plan designed to achieve your child's academic goals.

• Through our method of skill mastery, your child will not only learn and master every skill in his personalized plan, he will be truly motivated and inspired to achieve his full potential.

To get started, included with this Sylvan product purchase is $10 off our exclusive Sylvan Skills Assessment®. Simply use this coupon and contact your local Sylvan Learning Center to set up your appointment.

And to learn more about Sylvan and our innovative in-center programs, call 1-800-EDUCATE or visit www.SylvanLearning.com. *With over 1,100 locations in North America, there is a Sylvan Learning Center near you!*

5th-Grade Vocabulary Success

Copyright © 2009 by Sylvan Learning, Inc.

Published in the United States by Random House, Inc., New York, and in Canada by Random House of Canada Limited, Toronto.

www.tutoring.sylvanlearning.com

Created by Smarterville Productions LLC
Cover and Interior Photos: Jonathan Pozniak
Cover and Interior Illustrations: Delfin Barral

First Edition

ISBN: 978-0-375-43012-1

Library of Congress Cataloging-in-Publication Data available upon request.

This book is available at special discounts for bulk purchases for sales promotions or premiums. For more information, write to Special Markets/Premium Sales, 1745 Broadway, MD 6-2, New York, New York 10019 or e-mail specialmarkets@randomhouse.com.

PRINTED IN CHINA

10 9 8 7 6 5 4 3 2 1

Contents

Checking your answers is part of the learning.

Each section of the workbook begins with an easy-to-use Check It! strip.

1. Before beginning the activities, cut out the Check It! strip.

2. As you complete the activities on each page, check your answers.

3. If you find an error, you can correct it yourself.

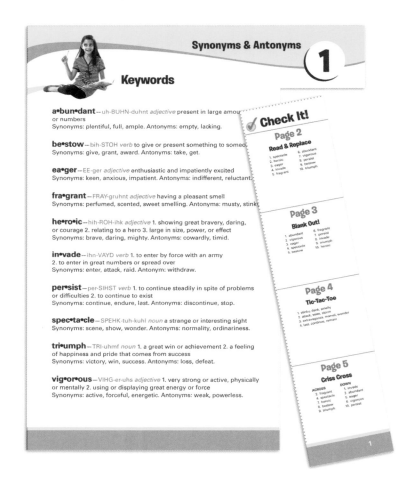

Keywords

a•bun•dant—uh-BUHN-duhnt *adjective* present in large amounts or numbers
Synonyms: plentiful, full, ample. Antonyms: empty, lacking.

be•stow—bih-STOH *verb* to give or present something to someone
Synonyms: give, grant, award. Antonyms: take, get.

ea•ger—EE-ger *adjective* enthusiastic and impatiently excited
Synonyms: keen, anxious, impatient. Antonyms: indifferent, reluctant.

fra•grant—FRAY-gruhnt *adjective* having a pleasant smell
Synonyms: perfumed, scented, sweet smelling. Antonyms: musty, stinky.

he•ro•ic—hih-ROH-ihk *adjective* 1. showing great bravery, daring, or courage 2. relating to a hero 3. large in size, power, or effect
Synonyms: brave, daring, mighty. Antonyms: cowardly, timid.

in•vade—ihn-VAYD *verb* 1. to enter by force with an army 2. to enter in great numbers or spread over
Synonyms: enter, attack, raid. Antonym: withdraw.

per•sist—per-SIHST *verb* 1. to continue steadily in spite of problems or difficulties 2. to continue to exist
Synonyms: continue, endure, last. Antonyms: discontinue, stop.

spec•ta•cle—SPEHK-tuh-kuhl *noun* a strange or interesting sight
Synonyms: scene, show, wonder. Antonyms: normality, ordinariness.

tri•umph—TRI-uhmf *noun* 1. a great win or achievement 2. a feeling of happiness and pride that comes from success
Synonyms: victory, win, success. Antonyms: loss, defeat.

vig•or•ous—VIHG-er-uhs *adjective* 1. very strong or active, physically or mentally 2. using or displaying great energy or force
Synonyms: active, forceful, energetic. Antonyms: weak, powerless.

 **Check It!**

Page 2
Read & Replace

1. spectacle
2. heroic
3. eager
4. invade
5. fragrant
6. abundant
7. vigorous
8. persist
9. bestow
10. triumph

Page 3
Blank Out!

1. abundant
2. vigorous
3. eager
4. spectacle
5. bestow
6. fragrant
7. persist
8. invade
9. triumph
10. heroic

Page 4
Tic-Tac-Toe

1. stinky, dank, smelly
2. attack, seize, storm
3. extravaganza, marvel, wonder
4. endure, continue, remain

Page 5
Criss Cross

ACROSS
2. fragrant
4. spectacle
7. heroic
8. bestow
9. triumph

DOWN
1. invade
3. abundant
5. eager
6. vigorous
10. persist

Synonyms & Antonyms

Read & Replace

READ the letter. The **bold** words are SYNONYMS to the keywords.
Synonyms are words that have the same meanings, like *big* and *huge*.

FILL IN the blanks with keywords from the word box.

| abundant | bestow | eager | fragrant | heroic |
| invade | persist | spectacle | triumph | vigorous |

Dear Jenna,

That was quite a 1 _____ you put on today. I had no
show

idea you were capable of such 2 _____ acts. I can't
brave

believe you were so 3 _____ to rescue us and put
keen

yourself in danger. Who could have predicted that a swarm of

bees would 4 _____ our lunch area? They must have
attack

been attracted to the 5 _____ flowers, or maybe it
sweet-smelling

was the 6 _____ amounts of perfume Counselor Kim
plentiful

was wearing. When I heard the buzzing sound, I crawled under

the picnic table. It was the most 7 _____ workout I've
energetic

had all summer! It's a good thing that you're not allergic to bees.

Amber said you had to really 8 _____ to get rid of all
keep going

the bees. The counselors are going to 9 _____ on you
award

the title of Camp Iwannagohome's Bravest Camper!

Congratulations on your 10 _____!
victory

Your BFF,
Marcus

Blank Out!

FILL IN the blanks with keywords.

1. Gail and Shanta always go fishing in April. The fish in Trout Lake are

    _____ in spring.

2. If you want to be an Olympic athlete, you will have to go through

    _____ training.

3. Evan was _____ to get to the beach before everyone else, so he

    woke up early.

4. The Fourth of July fireworks were a real _____.

5. The coach says he will _____ the honor of team captain on Dumont

    next season.

6. The _____ smell of cinnamon buns made Wendy hungry.

7. Juan was determined to _____ through the dance-a-thon, even

    though his feet were aching.

8. Angel spotted an army of ants that was about to _____ our picnic.

9. Finally jumping her bike over the ramp was a _____ for Deanna.

10. The firefighter who rescued the little boy did a _____ deed.

Tic-Tac-Toe

PLAY Tic-tac-toe with synonyms and antonyms. CIRCLE any word that is a synonym to the blue word. PUT an X through any antonyms. Antonyms are words that have opposite meanings, like *happy* and *sad*. When you find three synonyms or antonyms in a row, you are a winner! The line can go across, down, or horizontally.

HINT: If you find a word you don't know, check a dictionary or thesaurus.

Example:

bestow

give	award	take
obtain	grant	get
remove	withhold	present

1. fragrant

musty	perfumy	smelly
aromatic	dank	foul smelling
stinky	scented	sweet smelling

2. invade

withdraw	fall back	attack
raid	retreat	seize
vacate	overrun	storm

3. spectacle

event	normality	show
extravaganza	marvel	wonder
usualness	sight	ordinariness

4. persist

endure	stop	end
discontinue	continue	linger
quit	survive	remain

Criss Cross

FILL IN the grid by writing keywords that are synonyms to the clues.

ACROSS

2. Perfumed

4. Wonder

7. Mighty

8. Grant

9. Success

DOWN

1. Raid

3. Ample

5. Impatient

6. Forceful

10. Endure

Night & Day

MATCH each word in the moon column to its antonym in the sun column.

HINT: If you don't know the meaning of a word, look it up in a dictionary or thesaurus.

1. eager _____   a. cowardly

2. triumph _____   b. weak

3. vigorous _____   c. reluctant

4. bestow _____   d. defeat

5. persist _____   e. discontinue

6. fragrant _____   f. withdraw

7. spectacle _____   g. empty

8. invade _____   h. take away

9. heroic _____   i. stinky

10. abundant _____   j. normality

Blank Out!

FILL IN each blank with a keyword that is an antonym to the clue underneath.

abundant	bestow	eager	fragrant	heroic
invade	persist	spectacle	triumph	vigorous

1. We watched the crowd _____ the water park on the hot day.
   <u>leave</u>

2. May was exhausted after her _____ tennis match against Sue.
   <u>powerless</u>

3. Bees are attracted to the _____ smell of flowers.
   <u>stinking</u>

4. Lucy said we should all go to the concert tonight. It's supposed to be quite

   a _____.
   <u>humdrum event</u>

5. Victor's dad ordered an _____ supply of pizza for our party.
   <u>empty</u>

6. The mayor will _____ the key to the city on the winner at the
   <u>get</u>

   ceremony today.

7. Cassie was _____ to meet her favorite singer after the concert.
   <u>hesitant</u>

8. Raj's new role-playing video game is filled with _____ characters.
   <u>timid</u>

9. We're going out to celebrate Ivan's _____ at the chess competition.
   <u>defeat</u>

10. Kai knew he would

    _____ and get to
    <u>give up</u>

    the top of the jungle gym.

Petal Power

The petals around the flower are ANTONYMS to the word in the center. READ the words around each flower and WRITE an antonym in the center using the keywords.

abundant	eager	heroic	vigorous

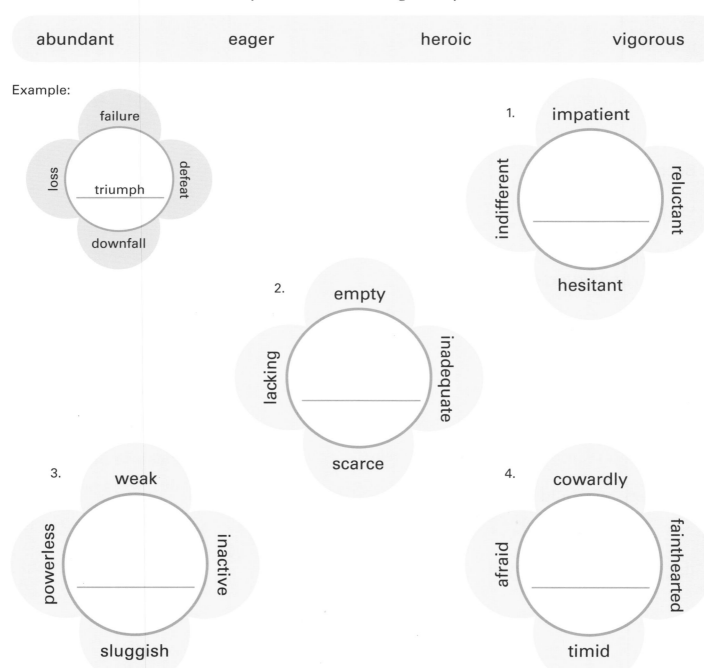

Example:

failure
loss — triumph — defeat
downfall

1. impatient
indifferent — _____ — reluctant
hesitant

2. empty
lacking — _____ — inadequate
scarce

3. weak
powerless — _____ — inactive
sluggish

4. cowardly
afraid — _____ — fainthearted
timid

✓ Check It!

Cut out the Check It! section on page 1, and see if you got the answers right.

Keywords

com•pre•hend—cahm-prih-HEHND *verb* to understand or grasp the meaning of
Synonyms: understand, get, perceive. Antonyms: misunderstand, mistake.

de•vour—dih-VOWR *verb* to eat up quickly and hungrily
Synonyms: gobble, gorge. Antonyms: fast, nibble.

e•merge—ih-MERJ *verb* 1. to come out into view, rise, or appear
2. to become known 3. to come to the end of a difficult or bad experience
Synonyms: rise, show, surface. Antonyms: fade, leave.

fa•tigue—fuh-TEEG *noun* extreme physical or mental tiredness
Synonyms: tiredness, weariness, exhaustion. Antonyms: freshness, energy, vigor.

har•dy—HAR-dee *adjective* 1. strong enough to survive difficult conditions
2. bold and daring
Synonyms: rugged, sturdy, strong. Antonyms: delicate, weak.

in•fe•ri•or—ihn-FEER-ee-er *adjective* 1. less important 2. of lower quality or value
Synonyms: low grade, shabby, lesser. Antonyms: best, superior.

lull—luhl *verb* to soothe or calm
Synonyms: soothe, calm, settle. Antonyms: disturb, alarm.

mis•for•tune—mihs-FAWR-chuhn *noun* 1. bad luck 2. an unpleasant or unhappy event or circumstance
Synonyms: misery, trouble, woe. Antonyms: luck, fortune.

sen•si•tive—SEHN-sih-tihv *adjective* 1. aware of other's needs, problems, and feelings 2. easily hurt or damaged
Synonyms: delicate, tender, touchy. Antonyms: heartless, insensitive.

with•er—WIH*TH*-er *verb* 1. to dry up or shrivel 2. to fade or become weak
Synonyms: droop, fade, shrink. Antonyms: bloom, grow.

✓ Check It!

Page 10
Read & Replace

1. emerge
2. hardy
3. comprehend
4. devour
5. lull
6. sensitive
7. wither
8. fatigue
9. inferior
10. misfortune

Page 11
Petal Power

1. emerge
2. fatigue
3. inferior
4. sensitive
5. wither

Page 12
Blank Out!

1. inferior
2. devour
3. misfortune
4. lull
5. sensitive
6. wither
7. comprehend
8. emerge
9. hardy
10. fatigue

Page 13
Criss Cross

ACROSS	DOWN
3. sensitive	1. emerge
4. comprehend	2. wither
7. fatigue	5. devour
8. hardy	6. inferior
10. misfortune	9. lull

Read & Replace

READ the e-mail. The **bold** words are SYNONYMS to the keywords. Synonyms are words that have the same meanings, like *happy* and *joyful*. FILL IN the blanks with keywords from the word box.

comprehend	devour	emerge	fatigue	hardy
inferior	lull	misfortune	sensitive	wither

From: Daisy Blossom
To: Meat-Eating Plants R Us
Subject: Tarantuplant

I am writing about the plant seed I ordered. In the beginning, I was very happy with your product. I watched the plant 1_____ **surface** from the soil. It grew and grew and soon appeared quite

2_____ **strong**. Unfortunately I did not 3_____ **understand** exactly how strong it would get. "Chewy" quickly began to

4_____ **gobble** everything in her path. It was all I could do to stop her from gobbling up my pets! They squeal and hiss at Chewy all the time. I've tried to 5_____ **soothe** them, but they're still upset. My rattlesnake is very 6_____ **delicate**, and now he won't come out from behind his rock! I don't want to see Chewy

7_____ **fade**, but I have to lock her in a closet. I'm suffering from 8_____ **exhaustion** trying to find enough food for her. May I please return her? I don't think your product is 9_____ **shabby** but I cannot handle any more 10_____ **trouble**.

Petal Power

The petals around the flower are ANTONYMS to the word in the center. Antonyms are words that have opposite meanings, like *up* and *down*. READ the words around each flower and WRITE an antonym in the center using the keywords.

emerge   fatigue   inferior   sensitive   wither

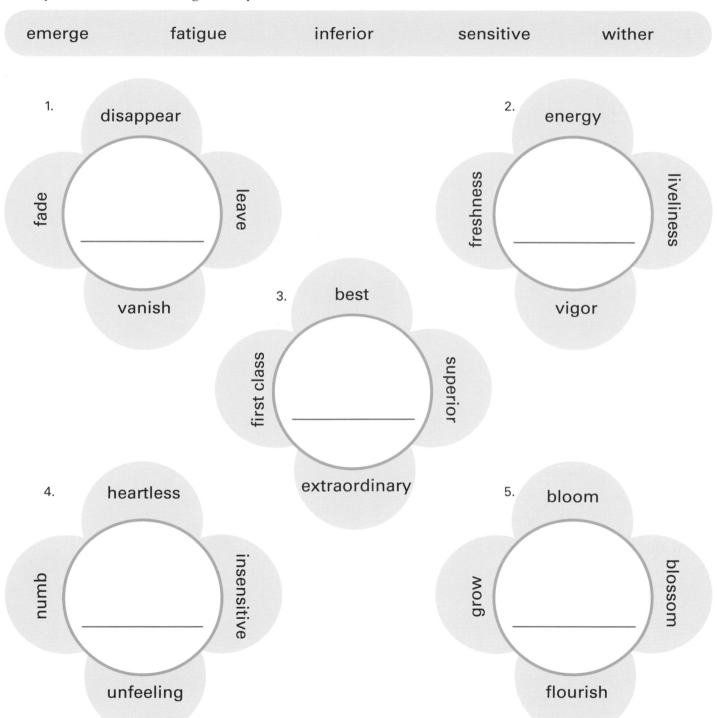

1. disappear
   fade   leave
   _____
   vanish

2. energy
   freshness   liveliness
   _____
   vigor

3. best
   first class   superior
   _____
   extraordinary

4. heartless
   numb   insensitive
   _____
   unfeeling

5. bloom
   grow   blossom
   _____
   flourish

Blank Out!

FILL in the blanks with keywords.

comprehend	devour	emerge	fatigue	hardy
inferior	lull	misfortune	sensitive	wither

1. The DVD was of _____ quality, so we returned it to the store.

2. Nat said he could _____ a whole chocolate cake by himself.

3. Lynette could not believe her _____ when she saw that her worst enemy had joined her cheerleading squad.

4. Baxter tried to _____ his baby sister to sleep, but she just kept on screaming.

5. Malik is a good person to talk to because he's so _____.

6. The beans will just _____ on the vine if we don't pick them soon.

7. Joy couldn't _____ why Beth would want to go parasailing on such a rainy day.

8. Carlo watched the butterfly _____ from its chrysalis.

9. Princess is a _____ dog. She likes to run around outside all day, even when it's freezing cold.

10. A nap might cure your _____ .

Criss Cross

FILL IN the grid by writing keywords that are synonyms to the clues.

ACROSS

3. Touchy

4. Perceive

7. Weariness

8. Rugged

10. Woe

DOWN

1. Rise

2. Fade

5. Gorge

6. Lesser

9. Settle

Tic-Tac-Toe

PLAY Tic-tac-toe with synonyms and antonyms. CIRCLE any word that is a synonym to the blue word. PUT an X through any antonyms. When you find three synonyms or antonyms in a row, you are a winner! The line can go across, down, or horizontally.

Example:

emerge

~~fade~~ X	~~disappear~~ X	~~leave~~ X
go away X	(surface)	(show)
(rise)	(appear)	vanish X

1. sensitive

tender	delicate	heartless
vulnerable	unfeeling	insensitive
emotional	thick skinned	touchy

2. wither

droop	fade	bloom
grow	blossom	shrink
flourish	shrivel	thrive

3. inferior

first class	foremost	best
mediocre	shabby	shoddy
second rate	poor	superior

4. hardy

robust	weak	tough
strong	sturdy	feeble
unhealthy	rugged	solid

Blank Out!

FILL IN each blank with a keyword that is an antonym to the clue underneath.

comprehend	devour	emerge	fatigue	hardy
inferior	lull	misfortune	sensitive	wither

1. The plants in your garden will _____ if you leave them out in
   flourish

   a frost.

2. If you are _____ to loud noises, you should move away from
   numb

   the speaker.

3. Kenny's trainer thinks he will _____ as one of the top runners in
   fade

   our town.

4. Only the most _____ athletes should sign up for the
   weak

   dogsled competition.

5. The singer tried to _____ the crowd so she could start her song.
   disturb

6. Hans had the _____ of watching his lunch get eaten by
   good luck

   hungry bears.

7. Yolanda's dad could not _____ what her text messages meant.
   misunderstand

8. The ancient sea monster could _____ a shark in one bite.
   nibble

9. You shouldn't buy that cell phone

   because it's _____
   superior

   to this new one.

10. _____ is one of
    Energy

    the symptoms of the flu.

Night & Day

MATCH each word in the moon column to its antonym in the sun column.

HINT: If you don't know the meaning of a word, look it up in a dictionary or thesaurus.

1. emerge _____
2. inferior _____
3. devour _____
4. lull _____
5. wither _____
6. comprehend _____
7. fatigue _____
8. sensitive _____
9. misfortune _____
10. hardy _____

a. weak
b. misunderstand
c. heartless
d. fade
e. better
f. luck
g. disturb
h. nibble
i. bloom
j. energy

 **Check It!**

Cut out the Check It! section on page 9, and see if you got the answers right.

Keywords

a•lert[1] — uh-LERT *adjective* 1. watchful and ready to face danger or emergency 2. active and brisk

a•lert[2] — uh-LERT *noun* 1. an alarm or warning of danger 2. a time of careful watching and readiness for danger 3. the period of time when an alert is in effect

ape[1] — ayp *noun* a chimpanzee, gorilla, or other tailless mammal in the same family

ape[2] — ayp *verb* to copy or imitate somebody or something

min•ute[1] — MIHN-iht *noun* 1. a period of 60 seconds or one sixtieth of an hour 2. a short period of time

mi•nute[2] — mi-NOOT *adjective* 1. very small 2. of little importance 3. marked by close attention to detail

sub•ject[1] — SUHB-jihkt *noun* 1. one who is under the rule of another 2. something that is being discussed, studied, or written about 3. an area of study

sub•ject[2] — suhb-JEHKT *verb* 1. to make someone go through an unpleasant experience 2. to bring under control 3. to expose to something

vault[1] — vawlt *noun* 1. an arched roof or ceiling 2. a secure room or compartment for keeping valuables 3. a burial chamber

vault[2] — vawlt *verb* to jump quickly or leap over

✓ Check It!

Page 18

Read & Replace

1. alert
2. ape
3. subject
4. minute
5. vault
6. minute
7. subject
8. ape
9. alert
10. vault

Page 19

Homograph Hopscotch

1. minute
2. subject
3. vault

Page 20

Blank Out!

1. alert
2. ape
3. vault
4. ape
5. minute
6. subject
7. alert
8. vault
9. minute
10. subject

Page 21

Double Match Up

1. e, p
2. h, s
3. g, q
4. a, j
5. c, t
6. d, r
7. f, o
8. i, l
9. m, n
10. b, k

Read & Replace

HOMOGRAPHS are words that have the same spelling but different meanings and sometimes different pronunciations. The *train* you ride and how you *train* your dog are homographs.

READ the story. FILL IN the blanks with keywords.

HINT: Read the whole story before you choose your words. Remember, each word has two meanings, so you can use it more than once.

alert	ape	minute	subject	vault

Something wasn't right at the zoo today. I noticed that the lions looked wide-eyed and 1_____. They're usually sleepy during the day. My brother and I saw a large furry 2_____. The animal thought it was funny to 3_____ people to flying banana peels. In the distance, I saw a 4_____ figure slinking around. I took out my binoculars and saw the ape's trainer 5_____ over the wall. She was only gone for a 6_____, and then she hopped back in again. I scribbled a note to my brother, and he ran off. The 7_____ of my note was the suspicious activity of the ape trainer. I realized that I was talking to myself when I saw a little boy 8_____ my gestures. "Scram!" I yelled. Suddenly the zookeeper blasted a bullhorn as an 9_____. Soon my brother came by with the police. The trainer had tried to break into a secret 10_____ underneath the ape house. Mystery solved!

Homograph Hopscotch

LOOK AT the definitions in each hopscotch board. FILL IN the matching keyword at the top of the board.

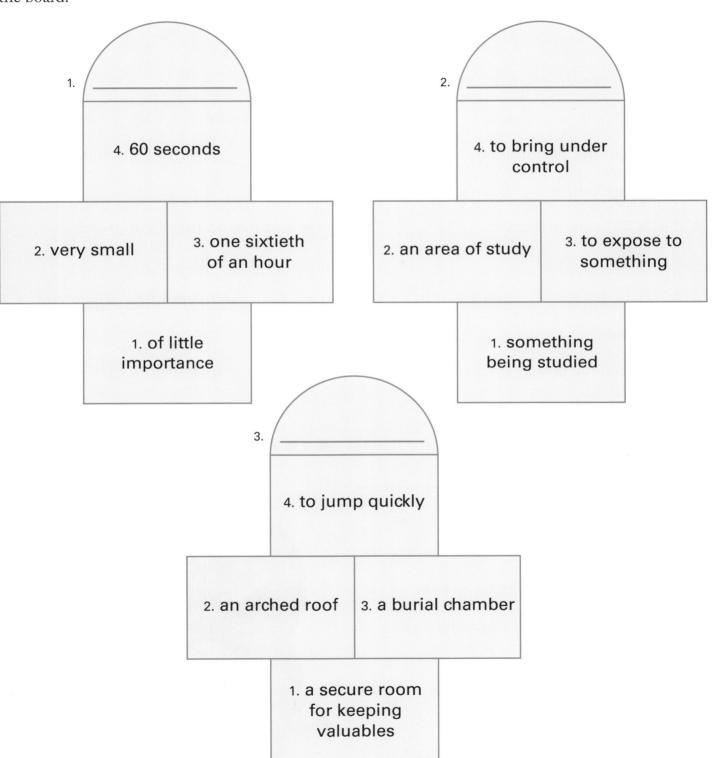

1. _____

4. 60 seconds

2. very small

3. one sixtieth of an hour

1. of little importance

2. _____

4. to bring under control

2. an area of study

3. to expose to something

1. something being studied

3. _____

4. to jump quickly

2. an arched roof

3. a burial chamber

1. a secure room for keeping valuables

Blank Out!

FILL in the blanks with keywords.

alert	ape	minute	subject	vault

1. The TV screen started flashing with a tornado _____.

2. The gorilla is an unusual _____ because it cannot easily climb trees.

3. Annie put her handheld game system in the hotel _____ while she went snorkeling.

4. Jack's little sister likes to _____ every move he makes. It drives him crazy.

5. A _____ can seem like a long time when you're standing on a stage by yourself.

6. I can't believe Greg's uncle wanted to _____ us to hours of his favorite polka CDs.

7. The lifeguard will _____ us if there is a dangerous riptide.

8. Gabby used a pole to _____ over the high jump bar.

9. This telescope is so powerful we can see _____ details on the moon.

10. Aliens and space invaders are the _____ of Hannah Lee's new book.

Double Match Up

FIND the two meanings for each word. Then WRITE the letters of the definitions that match the word.

HINT: If you get stumped, use a dictionary or thesaurus.

1. brace _____ _____

2. carp _____ _____

3. degree _____ _____

4. drain _____ _____

5. gorge _____ _____

6. mean _____ _____

7. lumber _____ _____

8. sheer _____ _____

9. story _____ _____

10. toll _____ _____

a. a pipe that carries water away

b. to ring a bell

c. to eat greedily

d. unkind

e. a support

f. to walk slowly

g. a unit of temperature measurement

h. a large fish

i. a thin fabric

j. to empty

k. a fee charged to use a road

l. straight up or down without a break

m. a short work of fiction

n. one of the levels of a building

o. wood

p. to prepare for something dangerous

q. a qualification given after finishing college or university

r. to have in mind or intend

s. to complain

t. a deep narrow valley

Criss Cross

FILL IN the grid by writing keywords that are synonyms to the clues.

ACROSS

4. An area of study OR to bring under control

5. An alarm OR active and brisk

DOWN

1. A short period of time OR very small

2. To leap over OR a burial chamber

3. To copy OR a member of the chimp family

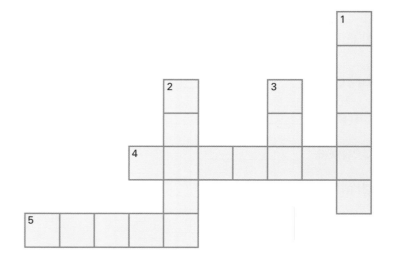

Double Trouble

WRITE the homograph that matches each description.

incline	express	impression	intent	spout	stall

1. Something planned OR focused on one thing _____

2. A booth set up to show goods OR to avoid doing something until later _____

3. A sloping surface OR likely to think or act in a certain way _____

4. The part of a container through which liquids can be poured OR to talk about something at great length _____

5. A mark left by pressing something hard into something soft OR a belief about something _____

6. To state thoughts or feelings OR traveling quickly _____

Write It Right

FILL IN the blanks by answering the clues with keywords. Then UNSCRAMBLE the letters in the circles to answer the riddle.

1. Why don't you stop in for a ___ ◯ ◯ ___ ___ ___ ?

2. Javier liked the acting, but he thought the ◯ ___ ___ ___ ___ ◯ ___ of the movie was boring.

3. We went to see the ___ ___ ___ ◯ ___ where the mummy was buried.

4. An orangutan is a type of ___ ___ ◯ .

5. Hilda's pet cat is most ___ ___ ◯ ___ ___ in the middle of the night.

Riddle

What is so fragile even saying its name can break it? ___ ___ ___ ___ ___ ___ ___

Blank Out!

FILL in the blanks with keywords.

alert	ape	minute	subject	vault

1. I know Justin thinks it's funny to _____ me, but I don't like it.

2. Zoe was excited to be the _____ of a newspaper article about kids who recycle.

3. It will only take Bella a _____ to dry her hair.

4. We can't believe that Tiny is going to try to _____ over that wall.

5. Did you see the hurricane _____ on the news?

6. The museum has even more paintings locked in a _____.

7. Pauline is a great table-tennis player because she's so _____.

8. The baboon is a monkey, not an _____.

9. There's a _____ amount of sugar left in the jar.

10. I hope Mei doesn't _____ me to her endless questions about my brother.

✓ Check It!

Cut out the Check It! section on page 17, and see if you got the answers right.

Just Right!

You've learned a lot of words so far. Are you ready to have some fun with them?

Synonyms may have similar meanings, but it's important to know which one is the right one to use in different situations. READ each sentence. Then CIRCLE the synonym that best fits the sentence.

1. TJ says she will give / bestow the comic book to me when she's finished.

2. We're waiting for the chick to rise / emerge from the egg.

3. Be careful with the crystal snowflake. It's sensitive / delicate.

4. Our refrigerator is full / abundant of food.

5. The wheels on that skateboard are inferior / low grade to these wheels.

Seesaw

LOOK AT the seesaws. WRITE a synonym on the level seesaws. Write an antonym on the slanted seesaws.

1. eager

2. triumph

3. wither

4. inferior

5. persist

6. hardy

Check It!

Page 25

Just Right!

1. give	4. full
2. emerge	5. inferior
3. delicate	

Seesaw

Suggestions:
1. excited
2. loss
3. shrivel
4. superior
5. stop
6. strong

Page 26

Pathfinder

1. inferior, superior
2. lull, alarm
3. fragrant, musty
4. heroic, timid
5. invade, withdraw
6. devour, fast

Page 27

Word Search

Double Trouble

1. ready to face danger
2. a large tailless mammal
3. 60 seconds
4. an area of study
5. to jump over

Pathfinder

Antonyms are opposites, and knowing your opposites can get you a long way in this game. Begin at START. When you get to a box with arrows leading you to two different boxes, follow the antonym to a new word. If you make all the right choices, you'll end up at FINISH.

Word Search

CIRCLE the homographs in the word grid. Words go across, up, down, or diagonally.

| alert | ape | minute | subject | vault |

B	V	A	C	A	J	O
V	A	P	P	L	M	I
S	U	B	J	E	C	T
U	L	B	L	R	T	I
P	T	J	V	T	L	U
M	I	N	U	T	E	M

Double Trouble

WRITE another meaning for each keyword.

alert: an alarm OR

1. _____

ape: to copy OR

2. _____

minute: very small OR

3. _____

subject: to bring under control OR

4. _____

vault: an arched roof OR

5. _____

Sniglets!

Would you like to make up a new word? You can start by making up a *sniglet*. Sniglets are fun-sounding words that use pieces of existing words. Here are some sniglets:

flopcorn—the unpopped kernels at the bottom of the microwave popcorn bag
pianope—refuse to practice the piano
weekdaze—the feeling you get when you can't wait for the weekend to come
snowbored—feeling tired of winter sports
rollerscrape—what you get when you fall off your roller skates
instrumeant—what a song is really about

WRITE a sniglet from the list to complete each sentence.

1. I wish spring would get here already because I'm so _____.

2. Haley read the song's lyrics to find out the _____, but they were too confusing.

3. Kevin took the popcorn out of the microwave too soon, so there was a lot of _____.

4. If you don't wear safety equipment at the skate park, you might get a _____.

5. Tasha said she was going to _____ because she wanted to play games instead.

6. Ling's _____ always starts on Wednesday afternoon.

✓ Check It!

Cut out the Check It! section on page 25, and see if you got the answers right.

Vive la France!

English is a funny language. Just when you think you've figured it out, there's something new to learn! That's because English is made up of many words from other languages. If you want to master those words, it can help to know where they came from!

Many English words that relate to law, government, and war come from French.

LOOK AT the French words. MATCH each one with an English word that looks similar.

French Words	English Words
1. parlement	a. chancellor
2. bataille	b. court
3. juge	c. defendant
4. soldat	d. government
5. chancelier	e. judge
6. compagnie	f. army
7. ennemi	g. soldier
8. gouvernement	h. parliament
9. armée	i. battle
10. défendeur	j. enemy
11. cour	k. company

Welcome to the Netherlands!

Did you have fun in France? Don't unpack your suitcase, because you're headed to the Netherlands.

The Netherlands is largely surrounded by water, so it's easy to understand why so many English words about shipping and the high seas come from Dutch.

LOOK AT the Dutch words. MATCH each one with an English word that looks similar.

Dutch Words	English Words
1. jacht	a. buoy
2. sloep	b. avast
3. lek	c. yacht
4. smokkel	d. cruise
5. boeg	e. dock
6. dok	f. pump
7. vracht	g. bow
8. boei	h. scour
9. pomp	i. sloop
10. scheuur	j. freight
11. houvast	k. smuggle
12. kruisen	l. leak

Welcome to Spain!

You may not know the language, but sometimes you can take a good guess. That's because many Spanish words will look very familiar to you.

LOOK AT the Spanish words. MATCH each one with an English word that looks similar.

Spanish Words	English Words
1. abundantemente	a. immediately
2. bulevar	b. reality
3. fabuloso	c. boulevard
4. generosidad	d. marvel
5. immediatamente	e. observe
6. maravilla	f. fabulous
7. naturalmente	g. naturally
8. observar	h. secretly
9. realidad	i. generosity
10. secretamente	j. abundantly

Words of Art

Japan's art forms have traveled all over the globe—and some are so popular that they have become a part of the English language!

MATCH each word to its definition by writing the letters in the blanks. If you see a word you don't know, grab a dictionary!

1. anime   _____   a. a very short 3-lined poem

2. bonsai   _____   b. artistic paper folding

3. haiku   _____   c. the art of creating and caring for miniature trees

4. karate   _____   d. Japanese comic books

5. karaoke   _____   e. Japanese animated films

6. manga   _____   f. singing along to recorded music

7. origami   _____   g. a method of self-defense using kicks and blows of the hand, not weapons

Keywords

a•board—uh-BAWRD *adverb* 1. on, onto, or into a ship or other vehicle
2. in or into an organization or group

a•bol•ish—uh-BAHL-ihsh *verb* 1. to put an end to something
2. to destroy

ab•sent—ab-SUHNT *adjective* 1. not attending or present 2. not existing
3. not paying attention

ab•sorb—uhb-SAWRB *verb* 1. to take in and make part of the whole
2. to soak up or suck in 3. to hold someone's attention

ad•just—uh-JUHST *verb* 1. to make small changes that make something
fit or function better 2. to adapt to a new setting or situation

ad•mire—ad-MIR *verb* 1. to like and respect very much 2. to have a high
opinion of

ad•ven•ture—ad-VEHN-cher *noun* 1. an unusual or exciting journey or
event 2. a task, trip, or project that involves danger and risk

ap•a•thy—AP-uh-thee *noun* a lack of interest, feeling, or emotion

a•shore—uh-SHAWR *adverb* on or to the land from the water

a•typ•i•cal—ay-TIHP-ih-kuhl *adjective* not the usual type or kind

✓ Check It!

Page 34

Match Up

absorb, c
ashore, g
adjust, a
apathy, d
adventure, b
atypical, f
aboard, h
absent, j
admire, i
abolish, e

Page 35

Tic-Tac-Toe

1. side, new, bridge
2. rupt, solve, normal
3. fix, little, ject

abbreviate	admission
abnormal	advance
abridge	advertise
abrupt	advice
absolve	alike
absurd	anew
address	aside
adhere	avoid

Page 36

Read & Replace

1. aboard
2. adventure
3. adjust
4. ashore
5. atypical
6. apathy
7. admire
8. abolish
9. absorb
10. absent

Page 37

Criss Cross

ACROSS	DOWN
1. apathy	2 aboard
4. absorb	3. ashore
7. adventure	4. adjust
8. atypical	5. absent
	6. admire
	9. abolish

Check It!

Match Up

PREFIXES are groups of letters that come at the beginning of a word. The prefixes "a-" and "ad-" mean *to*, *toward*, or *near*. The prefix "a-" can also mean *not* or *without*. "Ab-" means *away from* or *off*.

MATCH the prefixes in the box to the roots. WRITE each word and then MATCH it to its definition.

HINT: You can use each prefix more than once.

a-   ab-   ad-

sorb _____ ___

shore _____ ___

just _____ ___

pathy _____ ___

venture _____ ___

typical _____ ___

board _____ ___

sent _____ ___

mire _____ ___

olish _____ ___

Definitions:

a. to adapt to a new setting
b. an exciting journey to a place
c. to soak up
d. without feeling
e. to do away with or end
f. not the usual kind
g. to the land from the water
h. onto a ship
i. to have respect for
j. not present

Tic-Tac-Toe

PLAY Tic-tac-toe with prefixes. CIRCLE any root word that could be used with the prefix in blue. PUT an X through any word that could not be used with the prefix. When you find three X's or O's in a row, you are a winner! The line can go across, down, or diagonally. When you're done, make a list of all the words.

1. a-

turn	side	view
like	new	sell
believe	bridge	void

2. ab-

rupt	dress	topic
solve	sociate	breviate
normal	surd	school

3. ad-

fix	dress	vance
vertise	little	here
vice	mission	ject

Other Words Created with Prefixes

_____

_____

_____

_____

_____

Prefixes

Read & Replace

READ the story. FILL IN the blanks with keywords.

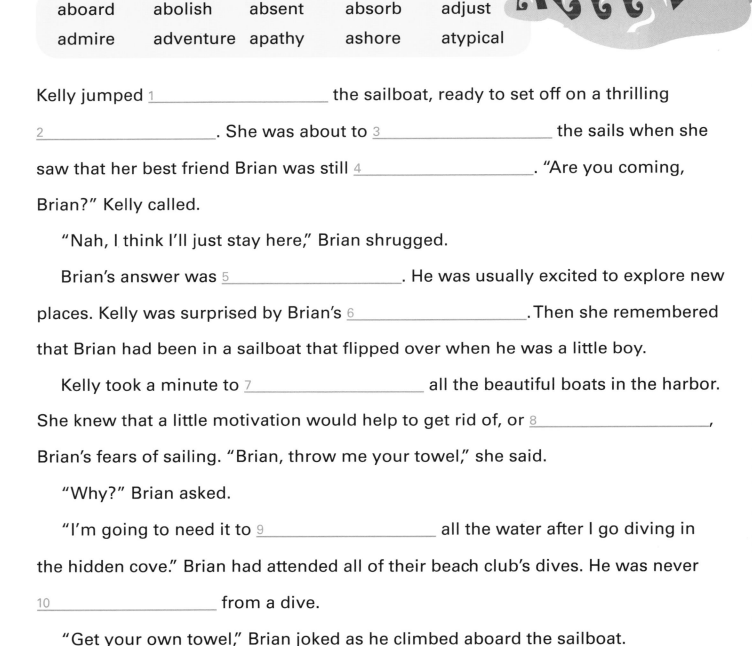

| aboard | abolish | absent | absorb | adjust |
| admire | adventure | apathy | ashore | atypical |

Kelly jumped 1_____ the sailboat, ready to set off on a thrilling

2_____. She was about to 3_____ the sails when she

saw that her best friend Brian was still 4_____. "Are you coming,

Brian?" Kelly called.

"Nah, I think I'll just stay here," Brian shrugged.

Brian's answer was 5_____. He was usually excited to explore new

places. Kelly was surprised by Brian's 6_____. Then she remembered

that Brian had been in a sailboat that flipped over when he was a little boy.

Kelly took a minute to 7_____ all the beautiful boats in the harbor.

She knew that a little motivation would help to get rid of, or 8_____,

Brian's fears of sailing. "Brian, throw me your towel," she said.

"Why?" Brian asked.

"I'm going to need it to 9_____ all the water after I go diving in

the hidden cove." Brian had attended all of their beach club's dives. He was never

10_____ from a dive.

"Get your own towel," Brian joked as he climbed aboard the sailboat.

Criss Cross

FILL IN the grid by answering the clues with keywords.

ACROSS

1. No interest

4. To hold someone's attention

7. A risky trip

8. Not like all the others

DOWN

2. Into a group

3. To the shore

4. To adapt to a new situation

5. Not present

6. To think highly of

9. To destroy

Prefixes

Blank Out!

FILL IN the blanks with keywords.

aboard	abolish	absent	absorb	adjust
admire	adventure	apathy	ashore	atypical

1. Naila was _____ from dance team practice because she had the flu.

2. If you _____ the straps on your backpack, it won't feel so heavy.

3. Beth watched her T-shirt _____ the dye.

4. When Dad found gum under the table, he said he was going to _____ chewing gum in the house.

5. Logan knew the rafting trip would be an incredible _____.

6. Victor's cat is _____. He likes to fetch sticks.

7. Deena found a message in a bottle that had washed _____.

8. I really _____ Sylvia's persistence.

9. Brenda's _____ towards the free candy is unbelievable.

10. Angel and I will have lunch _____ the ship.

It's Puzzling!

MATCH each prefix to a root word. Then WRITE the words in the blanks.

HINT: You can use the same prefix more than once. If you get stumped, use a dictionary.

a-

ab-

ad-

stract

drift

vert

dress

hor

dition

opt

_____

_____

_____

_____

_____

_____

Blank Out!

FILL IN the blanks with keywords.

| aboard | abolish | absent | absorb | adjust |
| admire | adventure | apathy | ashore | atypical |

1. When you just don't care one way or the other about the summer heat, it's called

   _____.

2. When a crab crawls out of the water, it is going _____.

3. It would be an _____ to go rock climbing with your friends.

4. If you are carrying your bags onto a ship, you are going _____.

5. I was _____ from tennis practice because I had too much homework.

6. If you look up to your big brother and want to be just like him, you

   _____ him.

7. If you dress differently than all the other kids your age, your sense of fashion

   is _____.

8. The cafeteria might stop serving French fries if they decide to _____

   junk food from the menu.

9. You can use a sponge to _____ the juice you've spilled.

10. If you shift your legs because the movie theater seat is uncomfortable, you

    _____ your position.

Keywords

con•cen•trate—KAHN-suhn-trayt *verb* 1. to focus attention or thoughts on one thing 2. to draw or bring things closer together 3. to take water out of

con•front—kuhn-FRUHNT *verb* 1. to face someone or something in challenge, to oppose 2. to cause to meet, to bring face to face with something

con•tem•po•rar•y—kuhn-TEHM-puh-rehr-ee *adjective* 1. happening, living, or existing at the same period of time 2. modern or current

con•ver•sa•tion—kahn-ver-SAY-shun *noun* a casual talk with somebody about feelings, ideas, or opinions

de•fend—dih-FEHND *verb* 1. to protect from harm or danger 2. to represent someone in court 3. to offer support for something or someone

de•part—dih-PAHRT *verb* to leave or go away from

de•press—dih-PREHS *verb* 1. to press down or cause to sink 2. to make someone sad 3. to decrease the value of

ex•hale—ehks-HAYL *verb* to breathe out

ex•port—ihk-SPAWRT *verb* 1. to carry away or remove 2. to send to another place for sale or exchange

ex•press—ihk-SPREHS *verb* 1. to state in words 2. to show thoughts and feelings through gestures, art, or drama

Check It!

Page 42
Read & Replace

1. concentrate
2. export
3. contemporary
4. depress
5. conversation
6. express
7. confront
8. defend
9. depart
10. exhale

Page 43
Petal Power

1. con-
2. de-
3. ex-
4. con-
5. de-
6. ex-

Page 44
Tic-Tac-Toe

1. form, done, dense
2. bug, code, feat
3. try, last, vend

concave	defeat
concourse	deliver
condense	exam
condone	explain
conform	expose
debate	extend
debug	extreme
decode	

Page 45
Criss Cross

ACROSS	DOWN
2. depress	1. depart
5. contemporary	3. express
7. conversation	4. confront
9. defend	6. concentrate
10. exhale	8. export

 **Check It!**

Page 46

Blank Out!

1. exhale
2. depress
3. export
4. confront
5. concentrate
6. contemporary
7. depart
8. defend
9. conversation
10. express

Page 47

It's Puzzling!

1. conclusive
2. confuse
3. control
4. convex
5. deforest
6. defuse
7. delay
8. excavate
9. exchange
10. exclusive

Page 48

Blank Out!

1. confront
2. exhale
3. export
4. contemporary
5. depart
6. depress
7. express
8. concentrate
9. conversation
10. defend

Read & Replace

Here are some more prefixes that can help you figure out the meaning of a word. The prefix "con-" means *with* or *together*. "De-" means *away* or *down*. "Ex-" means *out* or *from*.

READ the story. FILL IN the blanks with keywords.

concentrate	confront	contemporary	
conversation	defend	depart	depress
exhale	export	express	

Lena tried to 1_____ on her book, but she couldn't pay attention. All she could think about was Sam. They worked together in an 2_____ store that shipped boogie boards to other countries. They both loved to read the work of 3_____ poets. But they had their first fight, and it was starting to 4_____ Lena. She remembered their last 5_____. Lena just wanted to 6_____ her feelings. She felt like Sam never listened to her and that it was time to 7_____ the issue. But Sam got angry. Lena tried to 8_____ her position, but that only made things worse. She couldn't believe that Sam would ever 9_____ without saying goodbye, but he did. Lena took a deep breath and then began to 10_____. Then she picked up the phone and dialed Sam's number.

Petal Power

PREFIXES are added to root words to change or tell more details about the root. When you add the prefix "de-" to the root word *ice*, you make the new word *deice*, which means *to take ice away from*.

READ the word roots around each flower. Then WRITE a prefix that could be added to each root in the flower to make another word.

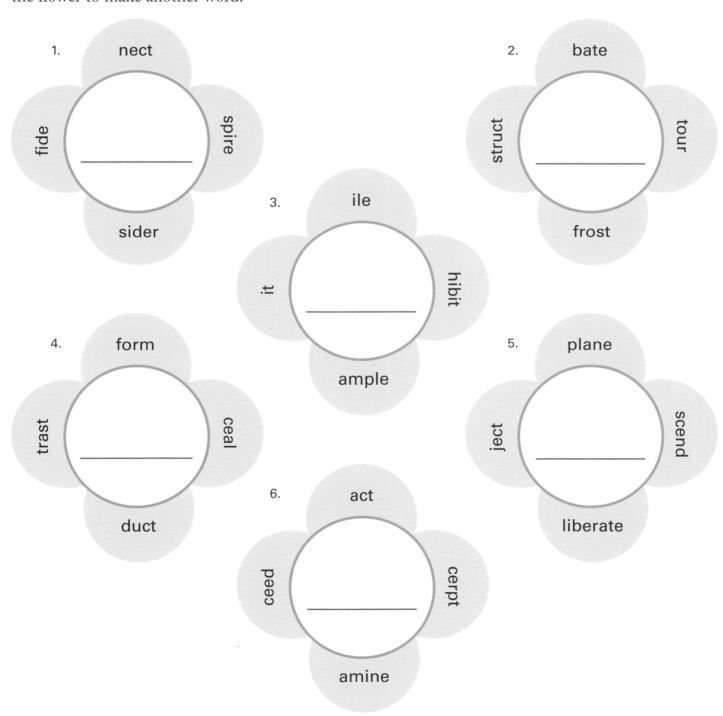

1. nect
fide
spire
sider

2. bate
struct
tour
frost

3. ile
it
hibit
ample

4. form
trast
ceal
duct

5. plane
ject
scend
liberate

6. act
ceed
cerpt
amine

Tic-Tac-Toe

PLAY Tic-tac-toe with prefixes. CIRCLE any root word that could be used with the prefix in blue. PUT an X through any word that could not be used with the prefix. When you find three X's or O's in a row, you are a winner! The line can go across, down, or diagonally. When you're done, make a list of all the words.

1. con-

judge	form	plan
cave	done	act
fell	dense	course

2. de-

bug	mind	bate
code	stand	found
feat	liver	win

3. ex-

try	plain	am
duct	last	tend
pose	treme	vend

Other Words Created with Prefixes

_____

_____

_____

_____

_____

_____

Criss Cross

FILL IN the grid by answering the clues with keywords.

HINT: Use the prefix meanings as a guide.

Prefix Meanings: con- = with, together   de- = away, down   ex- = out, from

ACROSS

2. Press **down**

5. Living **within** the same time period

7. A talk **with** someone

9. To drive danger **away**

10. To breathe **out**

DOWN

1. To go **away** from

3. To get your feelings **out** in words

4. To go face to face **with** someone

6. To draw things **together**

8. To remove **from**

Blank Out!

FILL IN the blanks with keywords.

concentrate	confront	contemporary	conversation	defend
depart	depress	exhale	export	express

1. Jamie could hold her breath for a whole minute before she had to

    _____.

2. You need to _____ the lever to get the toy out of the machine.

3. Hawaiian companies _____ surfboards to countries all over

    the world.

4. Kel knew he had to _____ the bully that was bothering

    his sister.

5. Hilda found it difficult to _____ on her routine with all the

    noise in the auditorium.

6. Matthew checked out the _____ fiction section to find a book

    by a current author.

7. The bus will _____ for the amusement park at 7 a.m.

8. Courtney will have to _____ her

    position during the debate.

9. Jalen and his mom were so absorbed in their

    _____ they didn't realize

    it was nearly midnight.

10. Sophia writes song lyrics to

    _____ her feelings.

It's Puzzling!

MATCH each prefix to a root word. Then WRITE the words in the blanks.

HINT: You can use the same prefix more than once. If you get stumped, use a dictionary.

con-   lay

de-   vex

ex-   cavate

fuse

trol

clusive

change

forest

_____

_____

_____

_____

_____

_____

_____

_____

_____

Blank Out!

FILL IN the blanks with keywords.

| concentrate | confront | contemporary | conversation | defend |
| depart | depress | exhale | export | express |

1. If you want to tell your dad why you're angry, you need to

   _____ him.

2. You have to _____ to blow up a balloon.

3. You might need to _____ your file onto a CD if you work on

   your friend's computer.

4. Mogul is a _____ style of skiing.

5. Will you wave goodbye when you _____ for summer camp?

6. You shouldn't watch a sad movie if it's going to _____ you.

7. You can use your smile to _____ happiness without saying

   any words.

8. If you _____ on the 3-D picture,

   you might see something surprising.

9. You can have a _____

   in person, on the phone, or by

   text message.

10. If your friend had a reason for being late,

    you might _____ him.

Keywords

ex•tra•cur•ric•u•lar—ehk-struh-kuh-RIHK-yuh-ler *adjective* activities that are outside the regular school or work routine

ex•traor•di•nar•y—ihk-STRAWR-dn-ehr-ee *adjective* better or beyond what is typical or regular, extremely good or special

ex•trav•a•gant—ihk-STRAV-uh-guhnt *adjective* 1. beyond what is reasonable or necessary 2. spending or costing an extremely large amount of money

o•ver•flow—oh-ver-FLOH *verb* to flood or flow over the brim or edge

o•ver•take—oh-ver-TAYK *verb* 1. to catch up with and pass by 2. to catch by surprise

o•ver•whelm—oh-ver-HWEHLM *verb* 1. to take over by greater strength, force, or numbers 2. to overpower in thought or feeling 3. to give a large or excessive amount of something to someone

su•per•in•ten•dent—soo-per-ihn-TEHN-duhnt *noun* 1. a person who manages the way work is done by a group or organization 2. a person who is responsible for taking care of a building

su•pe•ri•or—suh-PEER-ee-er *adjective* 1. better, above average 2. greater in quantity or number 3. higher in rank or importance

su•per•sti•tion—soo-per-STIHSH-uhn *noun* a belief in something that is not real or possible

su•per•vise—SOO-per-viz *verb* to watch over and make sure that a task or activity is being done correctly

 **Check It!**

Page 50

Read & Replace

1. extracurricular
2. overwhelm
3. superintendent
4. extraordinary
5. extravagant
6. overflow
7. superstition
8. supervise
9. superior
10. overtake

Page 51

Stack Up

EXTRA: terrestrial, galactic, sensory
OVER: grown, cast, joyed
SUPER: market, nova, hero

Page 52

Tic-Tac-Toe

1. active, board, look
2. bent, vect, look
3. hero, sonic, flow

extramural	overeat
extravaganza	overlook
extrovert	supercenter
overachieve	superfine
overactive	superhighway
overboard	superhuman
overcome	

Page 53

Criss Cross

ACROSS	DOWN
1. supervise	2. extravagant
5. extracurricular	3. extraordinary
6. overflow	4 superintendent
7. overtake	7. overwhelm
8. superior	

Even More Prefixes

✓ Check It!

Page 54

Blank Out!

1. extravagant
2. overwhelm
3. superstition
4. extracurricular
5. supervise
6. extraordinary
7. overflow
8. superior
9. superintendent
10. overtake

Page 55

It's Puzzling!

1. extracellular
2. extraneous
3. overcharged
4. oversleep
5. overstep
6. overworked
7. supercharged
8. superimpose
9. supertanker

Page 56

Blank Out!

1. superstition
2. overtake
3. supervise
4. extravagant
5. extracurricular
6. overwhelm
7. superintendent
8. overflow
9. superior
10. extraordinary

Read & Replace

READ the letter. FILL IN the blanks with keywords.

extracurricular	extraordinary	extravagant	overflow
overtake	overwhelm	superintendent	superior
superstition	supervise		

Dear Mr. Askalot,

We received your petition for a new 1_____ activity

for students who meet after school. The 100,000 names on your

list really did 2_____ me, so I shared your petition

with my 3_____. Unfortunately, while we agree that

a kayak run would be an 4_____ activity, the cost of

creating a river would be 5_____. There is also the

danger that during a storm, the river would 6_____.

Some people here believe the wacky 7_____ that

kayaks bring bad luck. Please submit a new proposal. I can

8_____ the program's development. Many believe

our neighboring town, Bestville, is 9_____ to

our town, and a great program might help us 10_____

their position of number 1 on the "Best

Places to Live If You Need a

Great After-School Program" list.

Sincerely,
Ms. Humdrum

Stack Up

LOOK AT the root words in the box. MATCH them with prefixes to make new words.

WRITE the new words under each prefix.

Prefix Meanings: extra- = outside   over- = too much   super- = more, better, higher

market	terrestrial	grown	galactic	nova
sensory	hero	cast	joyed	

extra-

_____

_____

_____

over-

_____

_____

_____

super-

_____

_____

_____

Tic-Tac-Toe

PLAY Tic-tac-toe with prefixes. CIRCLE any root word that could be used with the prefix in blue. PUT an X through any word that could not be used with the prefix. When you find three X's or O's in a row, you are a winner! The line can go across, down, or diagonally. When you're done, make a list of all the words. HINT: If you're not sure about some of the words, use a dictionary.

1. over-

achieve	call	active
come	cept	board
end	eat	look

2. super-

fine	dict	center
bent	vect	look
highway	human	flow

3. extra-/extro-

hero	sonic	flow
duct	vert	vaganza
mural	mand	ject

Other Words Created with Prefixes

_____

_____

_____

_____

_____

_____

Criss Cross

FILL IN the grid by answering the clues with keywords.

ACROSS

1. To make sure a task is being done correctly

5. Outside the regular school or work day

6. To flow over the brim

7. To catch by surprise

8. Higher in rank or importance

DOWN

2. Costing an extremely large amount of money

3. Extremely special

4. A person who takes care of a building

7. To overpower in thought or feeling

Even More Prefixes

Blank Out!

FILL IN the blanks with keywords.

extracurricular	extraordinary	extravagant	overflow	overtake
overwhelm	superintendent	superior	superstition	supervise

1. Rita's motorized scooter was an _____ present.

2. We're planning to _____ the other team with our powerful front line.

3. Zoe believes the _____ that four-leaf clovers are lucky.

4. Karate is Justin's favorite _____ activity.

5. Mr. Garcia asked Marisol to _____ the beach cleanup.

6. Amir has the _____ ability to pick up his guitar and play any song that he's heard.

7. Clark shouted when he saw the pool _____ into the yard.

8. Lin uses the expert trail because she is a _____ skier.

9. Brendan helped the building _____ shovel a path after the snowstorm.

10. If our team gets two more wins, we'll _____ the Bulldogs in the standings.

It's Puzzling!

MATCH each prefix to a root word. Then WRITE the words in the blanks.

HINT: You can use the same prefix or root more than once. If you get stumped, use a dictionary.

extra-

over-

super-

worked

impose

step

neous

cellular

tanker

sleep

charged

_____

_____

_____

_____

_____

_____

_____

_____

Blank Out!

FILL IN the blanks with keywords.

extracurricular	extraordinary	extravagant	overflow	overtake
overwhelm	superintendent	superior	superstition	supervise

1. If you think the number 13 is bad luck, you believe in a _____.

2. If you pass by the other runners on the track, you _____ them.

3. When you babysit your little brother, you have to _____ him.

4. Inviting 1,000 friends to your birthday party would be _____.

5. All the activities you do outside of school are _____.

6. If you swim in the ocean, a large wave could _____ you.

7. The _____ in your school makes sure the air conditioning is working on a hot day.

8. If you pour juice into a glass and it spills over the top, you have made it _____.

9. The ice cream at Frosty's is so delicious. It is definitely _____ to the one you buy in a store.

10. Snow in Death Valley is an _____ event. It's one of the hottest places on Earth.

Keywords

clar•i•fy—KLAR-uh-fi *verb* 1. to make clear or pure 2. to make understandable

com•put•er•ize—kuhm-PYOO-tuh-riz *verb* to organize, control, or produce something using a computer

dis•in•te•grate—dihs-IHN-tih-grayt *verb* 1. to break into small parts, pieces, or elements 2. to destroy the unity or wholeness of something

em•pha•size—EM-fuh-siz *verb* to give importance or draw special attention to something

fas•ci•nate—FAS-uh-NAYT *verb* to hold someone's interest or attention completely

in•i•ti•ate—ih-NIHSH-ee-ayt *verb* 1. to cause or start something to happen 2. to introduce someone to a new activity, skill, or area 3. to make someone a member of a group, organization, or religion through a special ceremony

le•gal•ize—LEE-guh-liz *verb* to make legal by making or changing a law

mod•i•fy—MAHD-uh-fi *verb* 1. to change slightly 2. to make less severe or extreme

nav•i•gate—NAV-ih-gayt *verb* 1. to find a course to follow and steer a vehicle there 2. to travel to water 3. to make one's way over or through

pu•ri•fy—PYUR-uh-fi *verb* 1. to remove harmful or unwanted substances to make something pure 2. to grow or become pure or clean

✓ Check It!

Page 58

Read & Replace

1. modify
2. computerize
3. emphasize
4. fascinate
5. clarify
6. navigate
7. purify
8. disintegrate
9. legalize
10. initiate

Page 59

Suffix Hopscotch

1. -fy/-ify
2. -ate
3. -ize

Page 60

Match Up

1. beautify
2. itemize
3. alphabetize
4. falsify
5. hydrate
6. alienate

Page 61

Criss Cross

ACROSS	DOWN
4. modify	1. clarify
7. disintegrate	2. emphasize
8. initiate	3. computerize
9. purify	5. fascinate
10. navigate	6. legalize

Suffixes

 **Check It!**

Page 62

Blank Out!

1. modify
2. navigate
3. disintegrate
4. emphasize
5. purify
6. computerize
7. fascinate
8. clarify
9. initiate
10. legalize

Page 63

Chopping Block

1. real
2. solid
3. captive
4. simple
5. class
6. accessory
7. active
8. type
9. civil
10. different

Page 64

Blank Out!

1. clarify
2. purify
3. computerize
4. emphasize
5. initiate
6. modify
7. legalize
8. disintegrate
9. navigate
10. fascinate

Read & Replace

A SUFFIX comes at the end of a word and has its own meaning. READ the letter. FILL IN the blanks with keywords.

| clarify | computerize | disintegrate | emphasize | fascinate |
| initiate | legalize | modify | navigate | purify |

Suffix Meanings: *–fy = make, do*   *–ize = make, become*   *–ate = make, cause*

Dear Editor,

I saw that you are going to 1_____ your magazine. It looks like you will 2_____ everything and publish a digital magazine. I want to 3_____ that there are paper lovers left. I know it's hard to believe that paper could 4_____ anyone, but it is true. Let me 5_____ my feelings. I find it difficult to 6_____ through the World Wide Web. My garage is full of old issues of *Rock, Scissors, Paper Illustrated*. I have designed a system to 7_____ the air so paper will not 8_____ over time. I am also working to 9_____ collecting magazines from other people's trash because it is against the law. I understand that you had reasons to 10_____ this process.

I hope you'll reconsider

your decision.

Your Loyal Reader,
P. T. Pulp

58

Suffix Hopscotch

LOOK AT the roots in each hopscotch board. FILL IN a suffix that can be added to all of the words in the board.

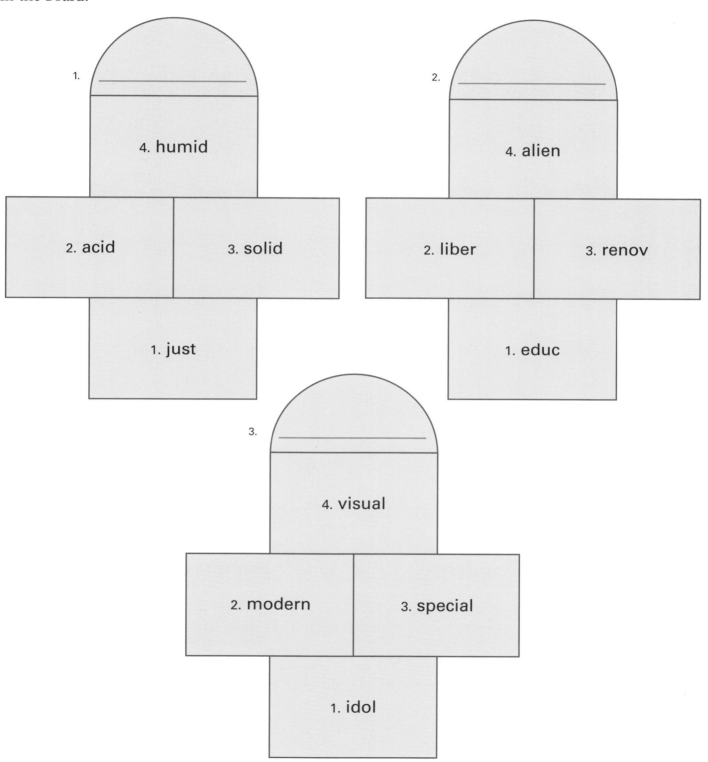

1. _____

4. humid

2. acid   3. solid

1. just

2. _____

4. alien

2. liber   3. renov

1. educ

3. _____

4. visual

2. modern   3. special

1. idol

Match Up

MATCH each root to a suffix. Then WRITE the word next to its definition.

HINT: Sometimes you drop or change a letter from the root word when you add the suffix.

Root

alphabet

alien

beauty

hydr

false

item

Suffix

-ate

-ize

-fy

-ate

-ize

-fy

Word   **Definitions**

1. _____   to make beautiful

2. _____   to make a list of details

3. _____   to put in alphabetical order

4. _____   to make false

5. _____   to supply with fluid or moisture

6. _____   to make unfriendly

Criss Cross

FILL IN the grid by answering the clues with keywords.

ACROSS

4. To make less extreme

7. To cause to break into small pieces

8. To make someone a member of a group

9. To become clean

10. To make a course and follow

DOWN

1. To make clear

2. To draw attention to

3. To produce with a computer

5. To hold someone's attention completely

6 To make legal

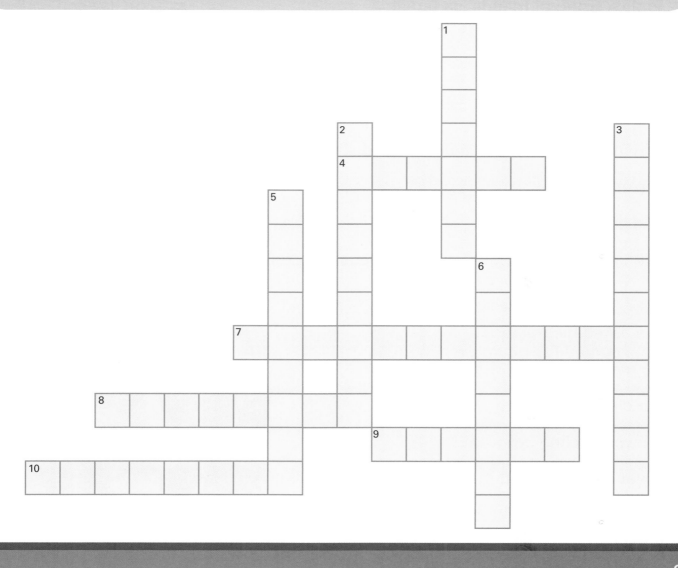

Blank Out!

FILL IN the blanks with keywords.

clarify	computerize	disintegrate	emphasize	fascinate
initiate	legalize	modify	navigate	purify

1. The coach showed Judith how to _____ her pitch so she could throw faster.

2. Vera and Leo brought maps to help them _____ through the woods.

3. Sonia's group of friends started to _____ as soon as she changed schools.

4. Keiko used a highlighter to _____ the important words in her letter.

5. Adriana brought a filter on her trip so she could _____ the drinking water.

6. Paul helped his mom _____ all the files in her office.

7. Donna didn't understand why the circus seemed to _____ so many people.

8. Dan asked his trainer to _____ the meaning of her instructions.

9. Our club is hoping to _____ a new recycling program.

10. Violet disagreed with her town's decision to _____ gambling.

Chopping Block

READ the words. CHOP OFF the suffix in each word by drawing a line right before the ending. WRITE the root word in the blank.

HINT: You may have to change or add a letter or two to make the root word.

1. realize   _____

2. solidify   _____

3. captivate   _____

4. simplify   _____

5. classify   _____

6. accessorize   _____

7. activate   _____

8. typify   _____

9. civilize   _____

10. differentiate   _____

Blank Out!

FILL IN the blanks with keywords.

clarify	computerize	disintegrate	emphasize	fascinate
initiate	legalize	modify	navigate	purify

1. If you don't understand what someone is saying, you need him to

   _____ it.

2. You can get a machine that will take dirt out of the air and _____ it.

3. When you use your laptop to keep track of your schedule, you

   _____ it.

4. If you slam your hand down while you speak, you want to _____

   what you are saying.

5. Some clubs like to _____ new members at a special celebration.

6. If you put a new seat and handlebar on your bike, you _____ it.

7. If you think people under 18 should be able to vote, you want them to

   _____ teen voting.

8. When you sit by a campfire, you can watch the burning wood

   _____.

9. Astronauts use computers to _____ through outer space.

10. If your friend says a book is so good you won't be able to put it down, he means it

    will _____ you.

Keywords

am•bas•sa•dor—am-BAS-uh-der *noun* 1. an important official sent to represent a country in a foreign place 2. someone who serves as an official representative of something

an•ces•tor—AN-sehs-ter *noun* someone from the past to whom a person is directly related, usually more distant than a grandparent

at•ten•dant—uh-TEHN-duhnt *noun* someone whose job it is to serve or help people

bi•ol•o•gist—bi-AHL-uh-jihst *noun* a scientist who studies living things

con•fi•dant—KAHN-fih-dahnt *noun* a person who is trusted with secrets

im•mi•grant—IHM-ih-gruhnt *noun* someone who has left his country to go live in another country

op•er•a•tor—AHP-uh-ray-ter *noun* a person whose job it is to run or control a machine

pac•i•fist—PAS-uh-fihst *noun* someone who is against fighting and wars

pe•des•tri•an—puh-DEHS-tree-uhn *noun* someone who travels by walking

phy•si•cian—fih-ZIHSH-uhn *noun* a doctor, someone who is qualified to practice medicine

✓ **Check It!**

Page 66
Read & Replace

1. confidant
2. ancestor
3. pacifist
4. immigrant
5. ambassador
6. biologist
7. physician
8. pedestrian
9. attendant
10. operator

Page 67
Suffix Hopscotch

1. –ian
2. –ist
3. -ant

Page 68
What Do I Do?

1. pedestrian
2. confidant
3. ambassador
4. immigrant
5. operator
6. biologist
7. pacifist
8. attendant
9. physician
10. ancestor

Page 69
Criss Cross

ACROSS	DOWN
1. pedestrian	2. immigrant
3. physician	4. confidant
5. ambassador	5. ancestor
6. pacifist	
7. attendant	
8. biologist	

More Suffixes

✔ Check It!

Page 70

Blank Out!

1. physician
2. immigrant
3. ambassador
4. attendant
5. pacifist
6. ancestor
7. biologist
8. confidant
9. operator
10. pedestrian

Page 71

Chopping Block

1. serve
2. violin
3. account
4. mathematics
5. guard
6. tour
7. Egypt
8. natural
9. type
10. occupy

Page 72

Blank Out!

1. physician
2. pacifist
3. ambassador
4. pedestrian
5. attendant
6. ancestor
7. biologist
8. confidant
9. immigrant
10. operator

Read & Replace

READ the story. FILL IN the blanks with keywords.

ambassador	ancestor	attendant	biologist	confidant
immigrant	operator	pacifist	pedestrian	physician

Suffix Meanings: –ant,   –ian,   –ist   =   *one who*

Dear Diary,

You are my only 1_____. I can't tell anyone else what I want to be when I grow up. There's so much pressure when you have an 2_____ who was the queen of Ancientia. She was a famous 3_____ who kept her nation out of war. My grandmother was the first 4_____ to move to the United States from her town. She worked hard and was eventually made the 5_____ to her homeland. Then there's my uncle, a famous 6_____ who discovered a new species of butterfly. And my older brother, a doctor, is the President's 7_____! I don't want to be any of those things. I'd like to be a crossing guard and just help a 8_____ cross the street safely. Or maybe a locker room 9_____ who brings water and towels to the athletes. I'd even be happy as the 10_____ of the cotton candy machine at the circus.

Thanks for listening,
Connie T. Ented

Suffix Hopscotch

LOOK AT the roots in each hopscotch board. FILL IN a suffix that can be added to all of the words in the board. HINT: You may have to change a letter of the root word.

1. _____

4. civil

2. library   3. music

1. veterinary

2. _____

4. active

2. geology   3. bicycle

1. cartoon

3. _____

4. account

2. assist   3. habit

1. inform

More Suffixes

What Do I Do?

MATCH each key word to a description. Then WRITE the word on the card.

ambassador	ancestor	attendant	biologist	confidant
immigrant	operator	pacifist	pedestrian	physician

1.
I walk around town.
_____

6.
I study living things.
_____

2.
You can tell me your secrets.
_____

7.
I believe war is wrong.
_____

3.
I officially represent my home country.
_____

8.
I serve people at the gas station.
_____

4.
I left my country to live here.
_____

9.
I can make you feel better when you're sick.
_____

5.
I control a big machine.
_____

10.
I'm your grandmother's grandmother's grandmother.
_____

Criss Cross

FILL IN the grid by answering the clues with keywords.

ACROSS

1. One who walks
3. One who practices medicine
5. One who represents a country
6. One who is against violence
7. One who serves or helps
8. One who studies living things

DOWN

2. One who went to live in a new country
4. One who hears secrets
5. One who someone is descended from

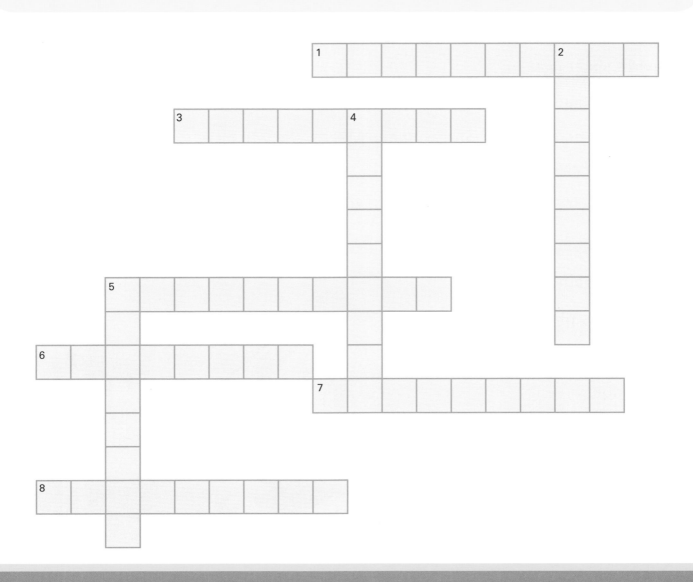

More Suffixes

Blank Out!

FILL IN the blanks with keywords.

ambassador	ancestor	attendant	biologist	confidant
immigrant	operator	pacifist	pedestrian	physician

1. Byron saw the team _____ after he twisted his ankle.

2. Igor and his parents are going to leave Russia to live here. He is

   an _____.

3. Ife's mother is the Nigerian _____. She works at the embassy.

4. Nicole got a summer job working as a pool _____.

5. David's sister is a _____. She believes it is wrong to fight.

6. Connor treasured the war medallion that belonged to his _____.

7. Amy loves plants, trees, and animals. Maybe she will be a _____.

8. Martin told Olivia all of his secret hopes and fears. She was his

   _____.

9. My dad's company is looking for an _____ who knows how to

   control a crane.

10. Our town is planning a new

    _____ lane for

    the bridge.

Chopping Block

READ the words. CHOP OFF the suffix in each word by drawing a line right before the ending. WRITE the root word in the blank.

HINT: You may have to change or add a letter or two to make the root word.

1. s e r v a n t _____

2. v i o l i n i s t _____

3. a c c o u n t a n t _____

4. m a t h e m a t i c i a n _____

5. g u a r d i a n _____

6. t o u r i s t _____

7. E g y p t i a n _____

8. n a t u r a l i s t _____

9. t y p i s t _____

10. o c c u p a n t _____

Blank Out!

FILL IN the blanks with keywords.

ambassador	ancestor	attendant	biologist	confidant
immigrant	operator	pacifist	pedestrian	physician

1. You need to see a _____ when you are sick.

2. You are a _____ if you believe you should figure out disagreements by talking rather than fighting.

3. If you need help in a foreign country, you can talk to our country's _____.

4. When you walk around town instead of driving, you are a _____.

5. The gas station _____ filled up our car.

6. Someone who lived a long time ago and is related to you is your _____.

7. The _____ studied bats and other cave-dwelling animals.

8. If you have a _____, it should be someone you trust to keep your secrets.

9. If your grandmother was born in a different country and moved away to live here, she's an _____.

10. It might be fun to work as the _____ of an ice-cream machine.

Pick the One!

Think you've got your prefixes straight? It's time to check your skills. LOOK AT each group of words. CIRCLE the real word in each row.

1. aboard   aport   amire

2. conpart   confront   conhale

3. debolish   detake   depart

4. extratypical   extraordinary extraflow

5. superior   supersent   superwhelm

6. overshore   overwhelm   overcurricular

7. export   exfend   exshore

8. adventure   adordinary   adpathy

9. abfend   absorb   abjust

Combo Mambo

WRITE all the words can you make by adding the prefixes to the root words.

| a- | ab- | ad- | con- | de- | ex- | over- | super- |

1. press _____

2. sent   _____

3. board _____

4. part   _____

Pick the One!

Now it's time to test your knowledge of suffixes. You know the rules—just CIRCLE the real word in each row. Ready, set, go!

1.	operatize	operatist	operator
2.	modist	modify	modize
3.	fascinian	fascinize	fascinate
4.	emphasify	emphasor	emphasize
5.	pacifize	pacifist	pacifor
6.	confidian	confidor	confidant
7.	pedestrian	pedestrior	pedestriate
8.	physicor	physisant	physician
9.	navigate	navigatist	navigatize
10.	purate	purant	purify
11.	biologor	biologize	biologist
12.	clarify	clarize	clarate
13.	ambassadant	ambassador	ambassadist
14.	disintegran	disintegrist	disintegrate
15.	ancestor	ancestist	ancestate

Pathfinder

Think you know your prefixes and suffixes pretty well? Then you'll have no problem with this game. Begin at START. When you get to a box with arrows leading you to two different boxes, pick the prefix or suffix that you can add to the root word. If you make all the right choices, you'll end up at FINISH.

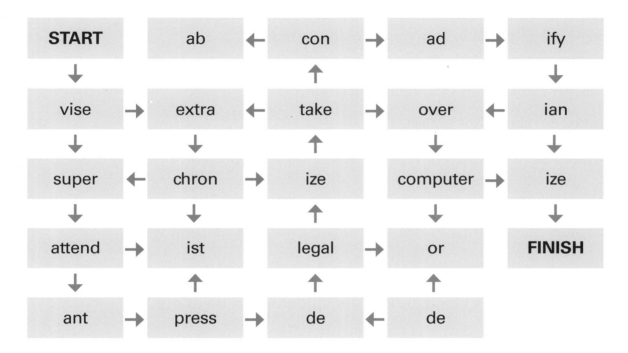

START	ab ←	con →	ad →	ify
↓		↑		↓
vise →	extra ←	take →	over ←	ian
↓	↓	↑	↓	↓
super ←	chron →	ize	computer →	ize
↓	↓	↑	↓	↓
attend →	ist	legal →	or	**FINISH**
↓	↑	↑	↑	
ant →	press →	de ←	de	

Sniglets!

Are you ready for some more sniglet fun? Here are sniglets made with prefixes and suffixes.

exaspirin—the impossible-to-remove cap on the pill bottle
magnifire—when you start something burning with a magnifying glass
maximonkey—the largest number of monkeys allowed at a zoo
minimunch—the least amount of food you can eat
supersnore—a snore that is so loud you wake yourself up
unfare—when the bus driver charges you too much

WRITE a sniglet from the list to complete each sentence.

1. The zookeeper said that six was the _____.

2. When Garth counted his change, he saw that the bus fee

   was _____.

3. Amy wanted something for her toothache and needed help with

   the _____.

4. Raj was trying to get a close look at the spider when he started

   the _____.

5. Julia couldn't get back to sleep after her _____.

6. Dad said that one bowl of cereal is the breakfast _____.

BONUS!

Now it's your turn. Here are some prefixes and suffixes you can use to create more sniglets.

WRITE DOWN your sniglets and their definitions.

Prefixes	Suffixes
ambi- = both	-oid = form, resembling
circum- = around	-itis = disease
endo- = within	-kinesis = movement
ultra- = beyond	-ship = state of being

_____

_____

_____

_____

Eat Your Words!

Many foods from other countries have made their way to our kitchens…and into our dictionaries. Can you guess where these foods come from?

MATCH each food to its plate.

China

Mexico

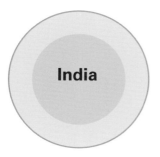

India

curry

bok choy

guacamole

chutney

chop suey

frijoles

won ton

tamales

naan

Yes, It's Yiddish!

Yiddish is a language that started in Eastern Europe and then made its way all over the world. Some Yiddish words landed in the English dictionary.

READ the definitions of each word. Then UNSCRAMBLE the answers.

1. A donut-shaped bread roll   ableg   _____

2. A clumsy person   lzutk   _____

3. A minor error, a slip   ctilhg   _____

4. To snack   snoh   _____

5. To make small talk   ozomhsce   _____

6. To carry or lug   pehcsl   _____

7. A comedy theme or routine   thicks   _____

8. Smoked salmon   oxl   _____

You Can Count on Arabic!

We use an Arabic number system, and many English words are borrowed from Arabic.

LOOK AT the Arabic words and their meanings. MATCH each one with an English word that looks similar.

1. *amir al-bihar*, commander of the seas   _____   a. gauze

2. *sifr*, zero   _____   b. alcove

3. *ardi chawki*, land thorn   _____   c. lime

4. *qazz*, raw silk   _____   d. monsoon

5. *limah*, a citrus fruit   _____   e. cipher

6. *matrah*, mat or cushion   _____   f. admiral

7. *mawsim*, season   _____   g. jar

8. *jarrah,* a vase   _____   h. magazine

9. *al-qubba,* the vault   _____   i. artichoke

10. *maxazin,* storehouses   _____   j. mattress

Time Travelers

Some words have traveled through time to get to the English dictionary. The words in the list below all came from Old Norse, a language that was spoken thousands of years ago in an area that spanned from Greenland to Russia. SEARCH the letters up, down, and diagonally to find words that came from Old Norse.

anger	from *angr*, meaning "trouble"
awe	from *agi,* meaning "terror"
blunder	from *blundra*, meaning "shut one's eye"
cast	from *kasta*, meaning "to throw"
crawl	from *crafla*, meaning "to claw"
haggle	from *haggen*, meaning "to chop"
oaf	from *alfr*, meaning "elf"
sleuth	from *sloó*, meaning "trail"
stagger	from *stakra*, meaning "to push"
whirl	from *hvirfla*, meaning "to go around"

Keywords

mag•nan•i•mous—mag-NAN-uh-muhs *adjective* showing kindness, generosity, or forgiveness towards someone

mag•nate—mag-NAYT *noun* a person who has earned a lot of wealth and power in a particular industry

mag•nif•i•cent—mag-NIHF-ih-suhnt *adjective* extremely good, beautiful, impressive, or fine

mag•ni•fy—MAG-nuh-fi *verb* 1. to make something appear larger than it is 2. to increase the size, effect, loudness, or intensity of something 3. to make something appear more important than it actually is

mag•ni•tude—MAG-nih-tood *noun* 1. great size, volume, or scale 2. the importance or significance of something

min•i•a•ture—MIHN-ee-uh-cher *adjective* smaller in size or scale than others of its type

min•i•mal—MIHN-uh-muhl *adjective* 1. very small or slight 2. the smallest or least possible

min•i•mize—MIHN-uh-miz *verb* 1. to reduce or keep to the lowest possible amount or degree 2. to intentionally underestimate the seriousness or extent of something

min•i•mum—MIHN-uh-muhm *noun* the lowest or smallest possible amount or degree of something 2. the lowest degree or amount recorded or allowed by law

mi•nor•i•ty—muh-NAWR-ih-tee *noun* less than half of a larger group

---

Read & Replace

ROOTS can be found at the beginning, middle, or end of a word. Each root has its own meaning. The root *magn* at the beginning of the word *magnificent* means *great*. The root *min* at the end of the word *miniature* means *small*. READ the story. FILL IN the blanks with keywords.

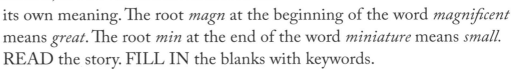

magnanimous	magnate	magnificent	magnify
magnitude	miniature	minimal	minimize
minimum	minority		

Judy looked at the secret potion. She thought it was

1_____ of her best friend to let her take the first sip.

Andy's mother was a 2_____ in the technology

industry. Cool, young people were in the 3_____ in

her office, so she was always bringing home new inventions for

Andy to test. The bottle was covered with crystals that seemed to

4_____ the liquid inside so it looked like there was an

enormous amount in the tiny container. Judy read the label. It said,

"Take a 5_____ five drops of this potion. Although

we have observed 6_____ side effects, we do not

know the 7_____ of this product's effectiveness." Judy

dropped five drops of potion onto her tongue. She held her nose

to 8_____ its bitter taste. At first, Judy felt

9_____. She was full of energy and power. Then she

looked up. Andy looked like a giant. Judy realized that the potion

had turned her into a 10_____ version of herself!

Root It Out

LOOK AT each definition. FILL IN the missing root letters.

HINT: The **bold** words give you a clue about the root.

Root meanings: magn = great, large   min = small, less

1. If you _____ify a bug, you make it look **larger** than it actually is.

2. The **lowest** speed allowed by law is the _____imum speed limit.

3. You are being _____animous when you show a **great** amount of kindness towards someone.

4. If **less** than half of your class plays guitar, then guitar players are in the _____ority.

5. You can _____imize your trading card collection and make it **smaller** by only keeping the cards that are really valuable.

6. If you've earned a **large** fortune selling ice cream, you are an ice-cream _____ate.

7. If you put **small** marshmallows in your hot cocoa, they are _____iature.

8. A _____ificent painting is one that has **great** beauty.

9. A very **slight** scrape is a _____imal injury.

10. The **great** size of an earthquake is its _____itude.

Combo Mambo

MATCH a word or ending in an orange box to a root in a yellow box to make a word. WRITE the word in the root box. Then LOOK UP the definition for each word and WRITE it in a sentence.

Root meanings: magn = great, large   min = small, less

ification	um	us	or	imalist	ificence

MAGN	MIN
_____	_____
_____	_____
_____	_____

_____

_____

_____

_____

_____

_____

_____

_____

_____

_____

Criss Cross

FILL IN the grid by answering the clues with keywords.

ACROSS

1. The lowest possible amount of something

3. Showing generosity towards another

4. To intentionally underestimate the seriousness of something

6. A person who has a lot of power in an industry

8. Less than half of a larger group

9. The importance of something

DOWN

1. The smallest or least possible

2. Very impressive

5. To make something appear more important than it is

7. Smaller in scale than normal

Blank Out!

FILL IN the blanks with keywords.

| magnanimous | magnate | magnificent | magnify | magnitude |
| miniature | minimal | minimize | minimum | minority |

1. Devan builds _____ furniture for her dollhouse.

2. We saw a _____ fireworks display after the parade.

3. Kids who dislike pizza are in the _____ in our class.

4. It was very _____ of Trevor to give the last cookie to his sister.

5. The theater requests _____ noise once the movie begins.

6. Sixteen is the _____ driving age in our town.

7. Amir's father started off with just one ship. Now he is a

   shipping _____.

8. Patricia's telescope can _____ the surface of the moon.

9. We didn't realize the play was going to be a production of

   this _____.

10. When Oscar goes water-skiing, he wears

    a helmet to _____ the

    risk of getting hurt.

It's Puzzling!

MATCH a prefix, root, and suffix together to form a new word. Then WRITE the words in the blanks.

HINT: You can use the same root or suffix more than once, and some words don't have a prefix at all. If you get stumped, use a dictionary.

Prefixes

di-

Roots

magn

min

Suffixes

-animity

-ute

-itud   -inous

-utive

_____

_____

_____

_____

Blank Out!

FILL IN the blanks with keywords.

| magnanimous | magnate | magnificent | magnify | magnitude |
| miniature | minimal | minimize | minimum | minority |

1. If you're the only one in your group of friends who wants to go skiing, you're in the _____.

2. When you make a problem seem bigger than it is, you _____ it.

3. If you _____ the amount of time you spend getting dressed in the morning, you can wake up a little later.

4. If you own popular lemonade stands across the country, you could be called a lemonade _____.

5. _____ horses are half the size of an average horse.

6. If your dad decides to forgive you for coming home late, he is being _____.

7. Most roller coasters have a _____ height requirement, and if you're shorter, they won't let you on.

8. Cody did a _____ jump in the half pipe. It looked like he could touch the clouds.

9. If your room isn't too messy, it will take a _____ amount of effort to clean it up.

10. If you think it's not a big deal to lie to your parents, you don't understand the _____ of what you've done.

Keywords

con•ces•sion—kuhn-SESH-un *noun* 1. the act of yielding or giving into someone or something 2. a special right or privilege given to someone

e•vac•u•ate—ih-VAK-yoo-ayt *verb* 1. to remove from danger 2. to empty

in•ter•cede—ihn-ter-SEED *verb* to come between two people or groups in order to settle a disagreement

pro•ceed—pruh-SEED *verb* 1. to go on or continue to do something 2. to move in a particular direction

re•cede—rih-SEED *verb* 1. to move away from or go back from a certain point or level 2. to grow less or smaller

se•cede—sih-SEED *verb* to separate or withdraw from an organization, including a country

va•cant—VAY-kuhnt *adjective* 1. not being used, lived in, or occupied 2. showing no signs of thought or expression

va•cate—VAY-kayt *verb* to leave, give up, or withdraw

va•ca•tion—vay-KAY-shuhn *noun* 1. a period of time for rest, travel, and recreation 2. a scheduled period when schools and businesses are closed

vac•u•um—VA-kyoo-uhm *noun* 1. a space that is empty of all matter 2. a device or machine that creates or uses a vacuum

✓ Check It!

Page 90
Read & Replace

1. evacuate
2. vacant
3. recede
4. vacuum
5. vacation
6. vacate
7. intercede
8. proceed
9. concession
10. secede

Page 91
Root It Out

1. evacuate
2. proceed
3. concession
4. vacant
5. intercede
6. vacate
7. vacation
8. secede
9. vacuum
10. recede

Page 92
Combo Mambo

CED, CEED, CESS
1. ceded: yielded or given by treaty
2. antecedent: something that happened or went before something else
3. precedent: following in time, order, or place
4. accessibility: capable of being reached

VAC
1. evacuation: the act of evacuating
2. vacantly: blankly, emptily
3. medevac: an emergency evacuation of the sick or wounded
4. vacuity: an empty space

Read & Replace

Here are some more roots to add to your collection. The root *vac* at the beginning of the word *vacant* means *empty*. The root *ced* at the end of the word *recede* means *go*. (You'll find the same root spelled differently in *proceed* and *concession*.) Read the story. FILL IN the blanks with keywords.

| concession | evacuate | intercede | proceed | recede |
| secede | vacant | vacate | vacation | vacuum |

Special Alert:

We need everyone to 1_____ the city zoo immediately.

We believed that the old snake house was 2_____, but

we were incorrect. This morning, we sent the janitor in to clean

up after the flood waters began to 3_____. Judging

from the way the janitor dropped his 4_____ cleaner

and ran away, we were wrong. The zookeeper is out of town on

5_____, and we are afraid the snakes will soon

6_____ the building and make their way out of the zoo.

We are looking for someone to 7_____ in this matter.

If you are a skilled snake handler, you should 8_____

to the zoo immediately. We are willing to make any

9_____ to resolve this matter, and we are offering

a large reward to anyone who can help us. We do need to be

sensitive to the snakes' needs, as the Zoological Society has

threatened to 10_____ from our Chamber of Commerce

if any snakes are harmed.

Root It Out

LOOK AT each definition. FILL IN the missing root letters.

HINT: The **bold** words give you a clue about the root. Some roots have alternate spellings.

Root meanings: ced, ceed, cess = go, yield   vac = empty, free from

1. If you e_____uate an area during a hurricane, you **empty** it and remove people from danger.

2. The parade will pro_____ when the band **goes** forward and heads down the street.

3. If you make a con_____sion and go to bed early so you can go to the movies on Saturday, you **yield** to your parents' request.

4. If the parking lot is **empty** of cars, it is _____ant.

5. If two of your friends are having a fight, you might inter_____ and **go** to talk to one of them about it.

6. When you _____ate your room, you go away from it and leave it **empty**.

7. If you are **free from** school for a week in the winter, you're on _____ation.

8. If our community decides to se_____ from the town, we will have to **go** and separately form our own township.

9. Outer space is a _____uum because it is **empty** of all matter.

10. When flood waters re_____, they **go** back to their original level.

Combo Mambo

FILL IN a root in each word. WRITE the word in the column with that root.
LOOK UP the definition. Can you see how it's related to its root?

Root meanings: ced, ceed, cess = go, yield   vac = empty, free from

_____ed

e_____uation

ante_____ent

_____antly

mede_____

pre_____ent

_____uity

ac_____ibility

CED/CEED/CESS	VAC
go, yield	*empty, free from*
1. _____	1. _____
2. _____	2. _____
3. _____	3. _____
4. _____	4. _____

Criss Cross

FILL IN the grid by answering the clues with keywords.

ACROSS

1. To continue to do something
3. A privilege given to someone
6. To leave
7. To empty and take to a safe place
9. A period of time when school is closed
10. To separate from an organization

DOWN

2. To grow smaller
4. To come between two groups to settle a disagreement
5. Not occupied
8. Empty space

Blank Out!

FILL IN the blanks with keywords.

concession	evacuate	intercede	proceed	recede
secede	vacant	vacate	vacation	vacuum

1. Zander likes to wait until the crowds _____ before he leaves the stadium after a game.

2. Lana and her friends like to play stickball in the _____ lot after school.

3. Every year Roger and his family practices how to _____ their home during a fire.

4. When you suck chocolate milk through a straw, you create a _____ in your mouth.

5. Christopher's family is going to the shore during summer _____.

6. The free after-school karate classes are a _____ for students who maintain a B average.

7. Patrick and his brother wouldn't stop arguing, so their parents had to _____.

8. The swim team has to _____ the pool by 10 p.m. on Friday.

9. Our band decided to _____ from the competition and hold our own Battle of the Bands.

10. Kyle wasn't happy that his parents were going to _____ with their plan to move to a new state.

It's Puzzling!

MATCH a prefix, root, and suffix together to form a new word. Then WRITE the words in the blanks.

HINT: You can use the same prefix, root, or suffix more than once. If you get stumped, use a dictionary.

Prefixes   **Roots**   **Suffixes**

in-   vac   -uee

_____

_____

_____

_____

e-   cess   -ant

ac-   -uator

-ible

Blank Out!

FILL IN the blanks with keywords.

| concession | evacuate | intercede | proceed | recede |
| secede | vacant | vacate | vacation | vacuum |

1. If you want your sisters to stop fighting, you should _____.

2. If there's absolutely nothing in your head at the moment, you might say it is

   a _____.

3. You might want to _____ the room if your little brother's

   tarantula escapes.

4. If you agree to wash the dishes so you can use the computer later, you are making

   a _____.

5. If you're not ready to _____ up the mountain, you need to take a

   break before you start climbing.

6. If your group decides to split away from another group, you are going

   to _____.

7. If your dad tells you to _____ the room so he can mop the floors,

   he means that you should leave.

8. When your next-door neighbors move out, their home will be

   _____ until someone else moves in.

9. You can watch the ocean waves _____

   at low tide on the nights after a full moon.

10. If the weather is good, you can go to the pool

    every day on your _____.

Keywords

chron•ic—KRAHN-ihk *adjective* 1. lasting a long time 2. always present or encountered

chron•i•cle—KRAHN-ih-kuhl *noun* an account or record of a series of events

chron•o•log•i•cal—krahn-uh-LAHJ-ih-kuhl *adjective* arranged in time order

chro•nol•o•gy—kruh-NAWL-uh-jee *noun* 1. the order in which events occur 2. a list or table of the times and the order in which a series of events occurred

cre•den•tials—krih-DEHN-shuhlz *noun* 1. achievements, training, and background that make a person qualified to do something 2. a letter or certificate that proves someone's position or qualifications

cred•i•bil•i•ty—krehd-uh-BIHL-uh-tee *noun* 1. the ability to inspire belief or trust 2. willingness to accept something as true

cred•it—KREHD-iht *noun* 1. praise or recognition for something achieved 2. a source of honor 3. a person's good reputation or influence

cred•u•lous—KREHJ-uh-luhs *adjective* 1. too ready to believe that something is true 2. resulting from a tendency to believe things too easily

in•cred•i•ble—ihn-KREHD-uh-buhl *adjective* 1. impossible or difficult to believe 2. amazing, unusually good or enjoyable

syn•chro•nize—SIHNG-kruh-niz *verb* 1. to happen at the same time 2. to make something work at the same time or rate as something else

✓ Check It!

Page 98
Read & Replace

1. chronic
2. synchronize
3. credentials
4. chronological
5. chronology
6. chronicle
7. credit
8. incredible
9. credulous
10. credibility

Page 99
Root It Out

1. chronic
2. credentials
3. chronicle
4. incredible
5. chronological
6. credit
7. credulous
8. synchronize
9. credibility
10. chronology

Page 100
Combo Mambo

CHRON
1. chronograph: an instrument for measuring time intervals
2. anachronism: something from another time wrongly placed in a historical setting
3. synchronicity: the quality of happening at the same time

CRED
1. credence: acceptance that something is true or real
2. creditor: a person owed money by another
3. discredit: to make someone appear untrustworthy or wrong
4. credible: having reasonable grounds for being believed
5. accredit: to give official authorization or approval

Read & Replace

Your collection of roots can grow even more!
The root *chron* at the beginning of the word *chronic* means *time*. The root *cred* in the middle of the word *incredible* means *belief*. READ the advertisement entry below. FILL IN the blanks with keywords.

chronic	chronicle	chronological	chronology	credentials
credibility	credit	credulous	incredible	synchronize

Late Again? Timekeepers Unlimited Is Here to Help!

Do you suffer from 1_____ lateness? Are you

unable to 2_____ the clocks in your home? Then

it's time for you to go to Timekeepers Unlimited. The founders

of our organization have the 3_____ needed

to officially assist you. We begin each meeting with a

4_____ account of the previous session. We

give our members a chart so they can keep a minute-by-

minute 5_____ of their day. Next week, our leader

will publish a 6_____ of our society's history. Our

members are a 7_____ to society. They show up

for every event on time. Their promptness is truly

8_____. This is not a gimmick. We are not trying

to squeeze money out of 9_____ people. You

can call the Excellent Business Bureau and ask about our

10_____. We'll set your clocks straight once and

for all!

Root It Out

READ each definition. FILL IN the missing root letters.

HINT: The **bold** words give you a clue about the root. Some roots have alternate spellings.

Root meanings: chron = time   cred = belief

| chronic | chronicle | chronological | chronology | credentials |
| credibility | credit | credulous | incredible | synchronize |

1. If you have a problem that lasts a long **time**, it is _____ic.

2. A doctor's _____entials help people **believe** that she is capable

   of doing her job.

3. An account that is written about events that happened over **time** is

   a _____icle.

4. If you find it hard to **believe** something, it is in_____ible.

5. If you put your e-mails in **time** order, they are _____ological.

6. If people give you _____it, they **believe** that you are worthy

   of praise.

7. If your best friend easily **believes** that everything you say is true, he

   is _____ulous.

8. If you and another drummer hit your drums at the same **time**, you

   syn_____ize your beats.

9. If people **believe** and trust in you, you have _____ibility.

10. When you make a list of the **times** and order in which events happened, it is

    a _____ology.

Combo Mambo

FILL IN a root in each word. WRITE the word in the column with that root.

LOOK UP the definition. Can you see how it's related to its root?

Root meanings: *chron = time*   *cred = believe*

_____ence

_____ograph

_____itor

dis_____it

ana_____ism

_____ible

ac_____it

syn_____icity

CHRON	CRED
time	*believe*

1. _____   1. _____

2. _____   2. _____

3. _____   3. _____

4. _____   4. _____

Criss Cross

FILL IN the grid by answering the clues with keywords.

ACROSS

2. Training that makes a person qualified to do something

7. In time order

8. Always present

9. Too ready to believe that something is true

DOWN

1. Recognition for something achieved

2. To make happen at the same time

3. The order in which events occur

5. The willingness to accept something as true

6. A record of events

7. Amazing

Blank Out!

FILL IN the blanks with keywords.

chronic	chronicle	chronological	chronology	credibility
credit	credentials	credulous	incredible	synchronize

1. Tasha wrote down her race times in _____ order to see if she had improve with practice.

2. Ed and Olivia will _____ their watches to be sure they start the competition at exactly the same time.

3. It's hard to trust in Tammy's _____ after she was caught making up stories for the school newspaper.

4. Garrett thought his new electric guitar was an _____ present.

5. Jack's mom used her _____ to get us backstage at the concert.

6. Violet is so _____ that you could tell her anything and she'd believe it.

7. The mayor gave _____ to the volunteer firefighters for saving the town hall.

8. Richard said he went for ice cream after the movie, but I saw him walk into the theater with a cone. There's something wrong with the _____ of his story.

9. Max is reading a _____ of a pioneer's journey across the country.

10. Flora stopped skating because of her _____ back pain.

It's Puzzling!

MATCH a prefix, root, and suffix together to form a new word. Then WRITE the words in the blanks.

HINT: You can use the same prefix, root, or suffix more than once. If you get stumped, use a dictionary.

Prefixes   **Roots**   **Suffixes**

ac-   cred   -ulous

_____

_____

_____

_____

ana-   chron   -it

mis-   cre   -ant

in-   -ism

Blank Out!

FILL IN the blanks with keywords.

chronic	chronicle	chronological	chronology	credibility
credit	credentials	credulous	incredible	synchronize

1. If someone tells you that you did a good job, they are giving you

   _____ for your hard work.

2. It's important for all the members of the dance team to _____

   their movements.

3. A trip to the moon would be an _____ experience.

4. If you write about what happens first, next, and last, you are describing the

   _____ of a story.

5. If you bite your nails every day, you are a _____ nail biter.

6. If you put your photos in _____ order, you organize them

   according to the time that they were taken.

7. It is easy to play a trick on someone who is _____.

8. A book that tells what happened over a period of time is a _____.

9. Your _____ tell someone if

   you have the training you need to do

   a job.

10. If people know that you always tell

    the truth, they will trust in your

    _____.

Keywords

an•ti•bi•ot•ic—an-tee-bi-AHT-ihk *noun* a drug or substance that is used to kill bacteria

as•pire—uh-SPIR *verb* 1. to seek to achieve a goal 2. to soar

bi•o•de•grad•a•ble—bi-oh-dih-GRAY-duh-buhl *adjective* capable of being broken down naturally

bi•og•ra•phy—bi-AHG-ruh-fee *noun* 1. an account of a person's life 2. the category of literature that refers to books about people's lives

bi•on•ic—bi-AHN-ihk *adjective* having ordinary human parts or functions replaced by mechanical devices

bi•o•sphere—BI-uh-sfeer *noun* the area of Earth where there are living things

in•spire—ihn-SPIR *verb* 1. to influence or motivate someone to do something 2. to bring about a particular feeling

per•spi•ra•tion—per-spuh-RAY-shuhn *noun* 1. the fluid that comes out of the body through the skin 2. the act of releasing the fluid

res•pi•ra•tion—rehs-puh-RAY-shuhn *noun* the act of breathing air in and out

spir•it—SPEER-iht *noun* 1. a special attitude or state of mind 2. a sense of enthusiasm and loyalty 3. a lively quality

✓ Check It!

Page 106
Read & Replace

1. biography
2. biodegradable
3. biosphere
4. perspiration
5 bionic
6. aspire
7. respiration
8. inspire
9. antibiotic
10. spirit

Page 107
Root It Out

1. respiration
2. biography
3. inspire
4. biosphere
5. biodegradable
6. bionic
7. perspiration
8 aspire
9. spirit
10. antibiotic

Page 108
Combo Mambo

BIO
1. biotechnology: the use of living things in industrial production
2. biopsy: the removal and examination of living tissue
3. biofuel: a fuel made from raw biological materials
4. biodiversity: the range of living things present in an environment

SPIR
1. conspirator: a person who joins in a group that secretly plots against someone
2. transpire: to become known or be revealed
3. aspirant: someone who hopes to attain something
4. uninspired: lacking originality or distinction

Read & Replace

The root *bio* in the middle of the word *antibiotic* means *life*. The root *spir* at the beginning of the word *spirit* means *breathe*. Read the letter. FILL IN the blanks with keywords.

| antibiotic | aspire | biodegradable | biography | bionic |
| biosphere | inspire | perspiration | respiration | spirit |

Dear Albert,

I have finally done it. Soon I will be so famous they will hire an author to write my 1_____. You know I have spent years trying to invent a 2_____ car that can later be turned into pig food. And you know, after that failed, I began to catalog all the living things in Earth's 3_____.

Well, you can forget about that project too. It took a lot of hard work (and some smelly 4_____), but I may have invented a 5_____ brain. You may wonder when I began to 6_____ to that goal. It began with my study of human 7_____. I wondered how the brain knew to tell the body to breathe. That thought began to

8_____ me to dig deeper into the brain. The only problem is that the brain is being attacked by a rare bacteria. My next goal is to create an 9_____ to stop the infection.

If you have any ideas, please let me know. I have always admired your pioneering 10_____.
Your friend,
Wan Tobefamous

Root It Out

READ each definition. FILL IN the missing root letters.

HINT: The **bold** words give you a clue about the root. Some roots have alternate spellings.

Root meanings: bio = life   spir = breathe

1. The process that makes you **breathe** is re_____ation.

2. A book about the **life** of a person is a _____graphy.

3. If you **breathe** life into someone's dreams, you in_____e them.

4. The area of the world where you can find **life** is the _____sphere.

5. Something that can be broken down by **living** things like bacteria is

   _____degradable.

6. A mechanical part that acts in place of a **living** organ is _____nic.

7. When you do something that makes you **breathe** heavily,

   per_____ation will appear on your skin.

8. When you a_____e to reach a goal, you put every **breath** you take

   toward reaching it.

9. Your enthusiastic team _____it is like **breath** of fresh air.

10. An anti_____tic is a drug that kills **living** things such as bacteria.

Combo Mambo

FILL IN a root in each word. WRITE the word in the column with that root.

LOOK UP the definition. Can you see how it's related to its root?

Root meanings: bio = life   spir = breathe

con_____ator

_____technology

tran_____e

_____psy

a_____rant

_____fuel

_____diversity

unin_____ed

BIO	**SPIR**
life	*breathe*

BIO	SPIR
1. _____	1. _____
2. _____	2. _____
3. _____	3. _____
4. _____	4. _____

Criss Cross

FILL IN the grid by answering the clues with keywords.

ACROSS

3. To soar

4. Able to be broken down naturally

5. The act of breathing air in and out

7. The whole area of Earth where there is life

9. The act of releasing fluids through the skin

10. A lively quality

DOWN

1. A drug used to kill bacteria

2. An account of someone's life

6. To bring about a particular feeling

8. Having human parts replaced by machines

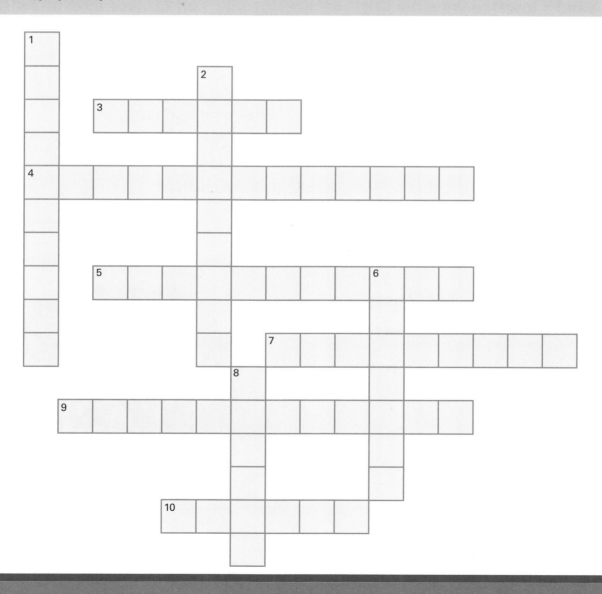

Blank Out!

FILL IN the blanks with keywords.

antibiotic	aspire	biodegradable	biography	bionic
biosphere	inspire	perspiration	respiration	spirit

1. I think that Lynn will _____ to be an Olympian.

2. Cathy thought about the view from the mountaintop to _____ her to climb higher.

3. Nat used a towel to wipe the _____ off his face after he finished the bike race.

4. Did you know plants give off oxygen during the _____ process?

5. Rita had to take an _____ when she had strep throat.

6. Lee is reading a _____ of the first woman to fly around the world.

7. The student government is holding a rally to boost school _____.

8. All the trees on Earth are part of the _____.

9. Wanda likes to use containers made out of _____ materials so they won't pollute the Earth.

10. Quincy is learning how to use his new _____ hand.

It's Puzzling!

MATCH a prefix, root, and suffix together to form a new word. Then WRITE the words in the blanks.

HINT: You can use the same prefix, root, or suffix more than once, and some words don't have a prefix at all. If you get stumped, use a dictionary.

Prefixes   **Roots**   **Suffixes**

a-   bio   -logy

_____

_____

_____

_____

auto-   spir   -graphy

re-   -ation

-atory

Blank Out!

FILL IN the blanks with keywords.

antibiotic	aspire	biodegradable	biography	bionic
biosphere	inspire	perspiration	respiration	spirit

1. A good beat can _____ you to get up and dance.

2. The paper you're writing on is _____.

3. If someone makes a movie about your life, it's your _____.

4. If you _____ to be a professional musician, you should practice as much as you can.

5. Your doctor might prescribe an _____ for an infection.

6. _____ can be a big problem if it leaks through your shirt.

7. Your lungs are the main organs you use for _____.

8. Scientists have developed a _____ leg that helps a runner keep up with professional athletes.

9. You are a living thing, so you are part of Earth's _____.

10. If you're always cheerful and full of enthusiasm, people will admire your _____.

Pick the One!

You know your root words, right? So get going and check your skills! LOOK AT each group of words. CIRCLE the real word in each row.

1.	magnitude	magnible	magniature
2.	overcede	intercede	decede
3.	biodulous	biocate	biodegradable
4.	abspire	inspire	prespire
5.	vacate	vacible	vacology
6.	minificent	minimal	minify
7.	chronicle	chronibility	chronable
8.	credulous	credant	credicle

Combo Mambo

WRITE all the words can you make by adding the suffixes to the roots.

HINT: Some suffixes can be used more than once.

Root	Suffix
bio	-ate
magn	-logy
chron	-ic
cred	-it
spir	
vac	

_____

_____

_____

_____

_____

_____

_____

Match Up

Can you MATCH each root word to its meaning? When you're done, WRITE three words that contain each root.

1. bio _____   a. believe

2. cede _____   b. less, little

3. chron _____   c. empty

4. cred _____   d. life

5. magn _____   e. time

6. min _____   f. go, yield

7. spir _____   g. breathe

8. vac _____   h. great, large

1. _____ _____ _____

2. _____ _____ _____

3. _____ _____ _____

4. _____ _____ _____

5. _____ _____ _____

6. _____ _____ _____

7. _____ _____ _____

8. _____ _____ _____

Pathfinder

The game's the same, only the roots change. Begin at START. When you get to a box with arrows leading you to two different boxes, pick the root that you can add to the prefix or suffix. If you make all the right choices, you'll end up at FINISH.

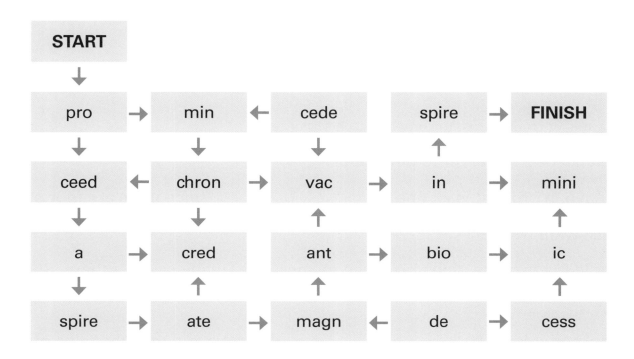

START				
pro →	min ←	cede	spire →	FINISH
ceed ←	chron →	vac →	in →	mini
a →	cred	ant →	bio →	ic
spire →	ate →	magn ←	de →	cess

Sniglets!

You're not quite finished with sniglets yet! Here are some sniglets made with root words.

overspiration—the heavy breathing you do when you exercise too much
telephony—someone who lies to you on a phone call
orchistruck—when a French horn falls on you
octopie—a circular food, like pizza, that is cut into eight slices
dinosore—something that's been hurting for a very long time
marathorn—a splinter that stays in your foot for 23 miles

WRITE a sniglet from the list to complete each sentence.

1. Warren needed a tweezer to pull out his _____.

2. We'll have to order at least one _____, since there are four of us and we each want two slices.

3. Jane told me that she didn't go to the movies, but Tiffany saw her there. She's such a _____.

4. We could hear Lenny's _____ all the way on the other side of the gym.

5. Marcus's head hurt after he was _____ during the concert.

6. Quentin couldn't remember the first time his neck started hurting. It was a real _____.

Now it's your turn. Here are some roots you can use to create more sniglets. Use what you know about prefixes, suffixes, and roots to write a definition for each. The sillier the better!

Root

aster = star	hypn = sleep
chrom = color	photo = light
cycl = wheel, circular	sequ = follow
dent = tooth	ultima = last
dynam = power	

_____

_____

_____

_____

a•board—uh-BAWRD *adverb* 1. on, onto, or into a ship or other vehicle 2. in or into an organization or group

a•bol•ish—uh-BAHL-ihsh *verb* 1. to put an end to something 2. to destroy

ab•sent—ab-SUHNT *adjective* 1. not attending or present 2. not existing 3. not paying attention

ab•sorb—uhb-SAWRB *verb* 1. to take in and make part of the whole 2. to soak up or suck in 3. to hold someone's attention

a•bun•dant—uh-BUHN-duhnt *adjective* present in large amounts or numbers. Synonyms: plentiful, full, ample. Antonyms: empty, lacking.

ad•just—uh-JUHST *verb* 1. to make small changes that make something fit or function better 2. to adapt to a new setting or situation

ad•mire—ad-MIR *verb* 1. to like and respect very much 2. to have a high opinion of

ad•ven•ture—ad-VEHN-cher *noun* 1. an unusual or exciting journey or event 2. a task, trip, or project that involves danger and risk

a•lert[1]—uh-LERT *adjective* 1. watchful and ready to face danger or emergency 2. active and brisk

a•lert[2]—uh-LERT *noun* 1. an alarm or warning of danger 2. a time of careful watching and readiness for danger 3. the period of time when an alert is in effect

am•bas•sa•dor—am-BAS-uh-der *noun* 1. an important official sent to represent a country in a foreign place 2. someone who serves as an official representative of something

an•ces•tor—AN-sehs-ter *noun* someone from the past to whom a person is directly related, usually more distant than a grandparent

an•ti•bi•ot•ic—an-tee-bi-AHT-ihk *noun* a drug or substance that is used to kill bacteria

ap•a•thy—AP-uh-thee *noun* a lack of interest, feeling, or emotion

ape[1]—ayp *noun* a chimpanzee, gorilla, or other tailless mammal in the same family

ape[2]—ayp *verb* to copy or imitate somebody or something

a•shore—uh-SHAWR *adverb* on or to the land from the water

as•pire—uh-SPIR *verb* 1. to seek to achieve a goal 2. to soar

at•ten•dant—uh-TEHN-duhnt *noun* someone whose job it is to serve or help people

a•typ•i•cal—ay-TIHP-ih-kuhl *adjective* not the usual type or kind

be•stow—bih-STOH *verb* to give or present something to someone. Synonyms: give, grant, award. Antonyms: take, get.

bi•o•de•grad•a•ble—bi-oh-dih-GRAY-duh-buhl *adjective* capable of being broken down naturally

bi•og•ra•phy—bi-AHG-ruh-fee *noun* 1. an account of a person's life 2. the category of literature that refers to books about people's lives

bi•ol•o•gist—bi-AHL-uh-jihst *noun* a scientist who studies living things

bi•on•ic—bi-AHN-ihk *adjective* having ordinary human parts or functions replaced by mechanical devices

bi•o•sphere—BI-uh-sfeer *noun* the area of Earth where there are living things

chron•ic—KRAHN-ihk *adjective* 1. lasting a long time 2. always present or encountered

chron•i•cle—KRAHN-ih-kuhl *noun* an account or record of a series of events

chron•o•log•i•cal—krahn-uh-LAHJ-ih-kuhl *adjective* arranged in time order

chro•nol•o•gy—kruh-NAWL-uh-jee *noun* 1. the order in which events occur 2. a list or table of the times and the order in which a series of events occurred

clar•i•fy—KLAR-uh-fi *verb* 1. to make clear or pure 2. to make understandable

com•pre•hend—cahm-prih-HEHND *verb* to understand or grasp the meaning of. Synonyms: understand, get, perceive. Antonyms: misunderstand, mistake.

com•put•er•ize—kuhm-PYOO-tuh-riz *verb* to organize, control, or produce something using a computer

Index

con•cen•trate—KAHN-suhn-trayt *verb* 1. to focus attention or thoughts on one thing 2. to draw or bring things closer together 3. to take water out of

con•ces•sion—kuhn-SESH-un *noun* 1. the act of yielding or giving into someone or something 2. a special right or privilege given to someone

con•fi•dant—KAHN-fih-dahnt *noun* a person who is trusted with secrets

con•front—kuhn-FRUHNT *verb* 1. to face someone or something in challenge, to oppose 2. to cause to meet, to bring face to face with something

con•tem•po•rar•y—kuhn-TEHM-puh-rehr-ee *adjective* 1. happening, living, or existing at the same period of time 2. modern or current

con•ver•sa•tion—kahn-ver-SAY-shun *noun* a casual talk with somebody about feelings, ideas, or opinions

cre•den•tials—krih-DEHN-shuhlz *noun* 1. achievements, training, and background that make a person qualified to do something 2. a letter or certificate that proves someone's position or qualifications

cred•i•bil•i•ty—krehd-uh-BIHL-uh-tee *noun* 1. the ability to inspire belief or trust 2. willingness to accept something as true

cred•it—KREHD-iht *noun* 1. praise or recognition for something achieved 2. a source of honor 3. a person's good reputation or influence

cred•u•lous—KREHJ-uh-luhs *adjective* 1. too ready to believe that something is true 2. resulting from a tendency to believe things too easily

de•fend—dih-FEHND *verb* 1. to protect from harm or danger 2. to represent someone in court 3. to offer support for something or someone

de•part—dih-PAHRT *verb* to leave or go away from

de•press—dih-PREHS *verb* 1. to press down or cause to sink 2. to make someone sad 3. to decrease the value of

de•vour—dih-VOWR *verb* to eat up quickly and hungrily. Synonyms: gobble, gorge. Antonyms: fast, nibble.

dis•in•te•grate—dihs-IHN-tih-grayt *verb* 1. to break into small parts, pieces, or elements 2. to destroy the unity or wholeness of something

ea•ger—EE-ger *adjective* enthusiastic and impatiently excited. Synonyms: keen, anxious, impatient. Antonyms: indifferent, reluctant.

e•merge—ih-MERJ *verb* 1. to come out into view, rise, or appear 2. to become known 3. to come to the end of a difficult or bad experience. Synonyms: rise, show, surface. Antonyms: fade, leave.

em•pha•size—EM-fuh-siz *verb* to give importance or draw special attention to something

e•vac•u•ate—ih-VAK-yoo-ayt *verb* 1. to remove from danger 2. to empty

ex•hale—ehks-HAYL *verb* to breathe out

ex•port—ihk-SPAWRT *verb* 1. to carry away or remove 2. to send to another place for sale or exchange

ex•press—ihk-SPREHS *verb* 1. to state in words 2. to show thoughts and feelings through gestures, art, or drama

ex•tra•cur•ric•u•lar—ehk-struh-kuh-RIHK-yuh-ler *adjective* activities that are outside the regular school or work routine

ex•traor•di•nar•y—ihk-STRAWR-dn-ehr-ee *adjective* better or beyond what is typical or regular, extremely good or special

ex•trav•a•gant—ihk-STRAV-uh-guhnt *adjective* 1. beyond what is reasonable or necessary 2. spending or costing an extremely large amount of money

fas•ci•nate—FAS-uh-NAYT *verb* to hold someone's interest or attention completely

fa•tigue—fuh-TEEG *noun* extreme physical or mental tiredness. Synonyms: tiredness, weariness, exhaustion. Antonyms: freshness, energy, vigor.

fra•grant—FRAY-gruhnt *adjective* having a pleasant smell. Synonyms: perfumed, scented, sweet smelling. Antonyms: musty, stinky.

har•dy—HAR-dee *adjective* 1. strong enough to survive difficult conditions 2. bold and daring. Synonyms: rugged, sturdy, strong. Antonyms: delicate, weak.

he•ro•ic—hih-ROH-ihk *adjective* 1. showing great bravery, daring, or courage 2. relating to a hero 3. large in size, power, or effect. Synonyms: brave, daring, mighty. Antonyms: cowardly, timid.

im•mi•grant—IHM-ih-gruhnt *noun* someone who has left his country to go live in another country

in•cred•i•ble—ihn-KREHD-uh-buhl *adjective* 1. impossible or difficult to believe 2. amazing, unusually good or enjoyable

in•fe•ri•or—ihn-FEER-ee-er *adjective* 1. less important 2. of lower quality or value. Synonyms: low grade, shabby, lesser. Antonyms: best, superior.

in•i•ti•ate—ih-NIHSH-ee-ayt *verb* 1. to cause or start something to happen 2. to introduce someone to a new activity, skill, or area 3. to make someone a member of a group, organization, or religion through a special ceremony

in•spire—ihn-SPIR *verb* 1. to influence or motivate someone to do something 2. to bring about a particular feeling

in•ter•cede—ihn-ter-SEED *verb* to come between two people or groups in order to settle a disagreement

in•vade—ihn-VAYD *verb* 1. to enter by force with an army 2. to enter in great numbers or spread over. Synonyms: enter, attack, raid. Antonym: withdraw.

le•gal•ize—LEE-guh-liz *verb* to make legal by making or changing a law

lull—luhl *verb* to soothe or calm. Synonyms: soothe, calm, settle. Antonyms: disturb, alarm.

mag•nan•i•mous—mag-NAN-uh-muhs *adjective* showing kindness, generosity, or forgiveness towards someone

mag•nate—mag-NAYT *noun* a person who has earned a lot of wealth and power in a particular industry

mag•nif•i•cent—mag-NIHF-ih-suhnt *adjective* extremely good, beautiful, impressive, or fine

mag•ni•fy—MAG-nuh-fi *verb* 1. to make something appear larger than it is 2. to increase the size, effect, loudness, or intensity of something 3. to make something appear more important than it actually is

mag•ni•tude—MAG-nih-tood *noun* 1. great size, volume, or scale 2. the importance or significance of something

min•i•a•ture—MIHN-ee-uh-cher *adjective* smaller in size or scale than others of its type

min•i•mal—MIHN-uh-muhl *adjective* 1. very small or slight 2. the smallest or least possible

min•i•mize—MIHN-uh-miz *verb* 1. to reduce or keep to the lowest possible amount or degree 2. to intentionally underestimate the seriousness or extent of something

min•i•mum—MIHN-uh-muhm *noun* the lowest or smallest possible amount or degree of something 2. the lowest degree or amount recorded or allowed by law

mi•nor•i•ty—muh-NAWR-ih-tee *noun* less than half of a larger group

min•ute^1—MIHN-iht *noun* 1. a period of 60 seconds or one sixtieth of an hour 2. a short period of time

mi•nute^2—mi-NOOT *adjective* 1. very small 2. of little importance 3. marked by close attention to detail

mis•for•tune—mihs-FAWR-chuhn *noun* 1. bad luck 2. an unpleasant or unhappy event or circumstance. Synonyms: misery, trouble, woe. Antonyms: luck, fortune.

mod•i•fy—MAHD-uh-fi *verb* 1. to change slightly 2. to make less severe or extreme

nav•i•gate—NAV-ih-gayt *verb* 1. to find a course to follow and steer a vehicle there 2. to travel to water 3. to make one's way over or through

op•er•a•tor—AHP-uh-ray-ter *noun* a person whose job it is to run or control a machine

o•ver•flow—oh-ver-FLOH *verb* to flood or flow over the brim or edge

o•ver•take—oh-ver-TAYK *verb* 1. to catch up with and pass by 2. to catch by surprise

o•ver•whelm—oh-ver-HWEHLM *verb* 1. to take over by greater strength, force, or numbers 2. to overpower in thought or feeling 3. to give a large or excessive amount of something to someone

pac•i•fist—PAS-uh-fihst *noun* someone who is against fighting and wars

Index

pe•des•tri•an—puh-DEHS-tree-uhn *noun* someone who travels by walking

per•sist—per-SIHST *verb* 1. to continue steadily in spite of problems or difficulties 2. to continue to exist. Synonyms: continue, endure, last. Antonyms: discontinue, stop.

per•spi•ra•tion—per-spuh-RAY-shuhn *noun* 1. the fluid that comes out of the body through the skin 2. the act of releasing the fluid

phy•si•cian—fih-ZIHSH-uhn *noun* a doctor, someone who is qualified to practice medicine

pro•ceed—pruh-SEED *verb* 1. to go on or continue to do something 2. to move in a particular direction

pu•ri•fy—PYUR-uh-fi *verb* 1. to remove harmful or unwanted substances to make something pure 2. to grow or become pure or clean

re•cede—rih-SEED *verb* 1. to move away from or go back from a certain point or level 2. to grow less or smaller

res•pi•ra•tion—rehs-puh-RAY-shuhn *noun* the act of breathing air in and out

se•cede—sih-SEED *verb* to separate or withdraw from an organization, including a country

sen•si•tive—SEHN-sih-tihv *adjective* 1. aware of other's needs, problems, and feelings 2. easily hurt or damaged. Synonyms: delicate, tender, touchy. Antonyms: heartless, insensitive.

spec•ta•cle—SPEHK-tuh-kuhl *noun* a strange or interesting sight. Synonyms: scene, show, wonder. Antonyms: normality, ordinariness.

spir•it—SPEER-iht *noun* 1. a special attitude or state of mind 2. a sense of enthusiasm and loyalty 3. a lively quality

sub•ject¹—SUHB-jihkt *noun* 1. one who is under the rule of another 2. something that is being discussed, studied, or written about 3. an area of study

sub•ject²—suhb-JEHKT *verb* 1. to make someone go through an unpleasant experience 2. to bring under control 3. to expose to something

su•per•in•ten•dent—soo-per-ihn-TEHN-duhnt *noun* 1. a person who manages the way work is done by a group or organization 2. a person who is responsible for taking care of a building

su•pe•ri•or—*suh-PEER-ee-er adjective* 1. better, above average 2. greater in quantity or number 3. higher in rank or importance

su•per•sti•tion—soo-per-STIHSH-uhn *noun* a belief in something that is not real or possible

su•per•vise—SOO-per-viz *verb* to watch over and make sure that a task or activity is being done correctly

syn•chro•nize—SIHNG-kruh-niz *verb* 1. to happen at the same time 2. to make something work at the same time or rate as something else

tri•umph—TRI-uhmf *noun* 1. a great win or achievement 2. a feeling of happiness and pride that comes from success. Synonyms: victory, win, success. Antonyms: loss, defeat.

va•cant—VAY-kuhnt *adjective* 1. not being used, lived in, or occupied 2. showing no signs of thought or expression

va•cate—VAY-kayt *verb* to leave, give up, or withdraw

va•ca•tion—vay-KAY-shuhn *noun* 1. a period of time for rest, travel, and recreation 2. a scheduled period when schools and businesses are closed

vac•u•um—VA-kyoo-uhm *noun* 1. a space that is empty of all matter 2. a device or machine that creates or uses a vacuum

vault¹—vawlt *noun* 1. an arched roof or ceiling 2. a secure room or compartment for keeping valuables 3. a burial chamber

vault²—vawlt *verb* to jump quickly or leap over

vig•or•ous—VIHG-er-uhs *adjective* 1. very strong or active, physically or mentally 2. using or displaying great energy or force. Synonyms: active, forceful, energetic. Antonyms: weak, powerless.

with•er—WIH*TH*-er *verb* 1. to dry up or shrivel 2. to fade or become weak. Synonyms: droop, fade, shrink. Antonyms: bloom, grow.